CONTENTS

INTRODUCTION
100 Literacy Framework Lessons: Year 2

About the series

The *100 Literacy Framework Lessons* series is a response to the Primary National Strategy's revised Literacy Framework and contains **all new** material. The lessons mirror the structure and learning objectives of the Exemplification Units of the Framework. The CD-ROM provides appropriate and exciting texts and also contains a variety of other resources from videos and images to audio and weblinks, which will help to guide you in implementing the Framework's emphasis on ICT texts. The books and CD-ROMs will be an invaluable resource to help you understand and implement the revised Framework.

The key points of the revised framework are:

- The development of early reading and phonics;
- Coherent and progressive teaching of word-level and sentence-level embedded into learning or taught discretely;
- Following and building upon the teaching sequence from reading to writing and developing comprehension;
- Flexible lessons providing a challenging pace;
- Integration of speaking and listening skills;
- Planning for inclusion;
- Broadening and strengthening pedagogy.

Early reading and phonics

The authors of the *100 Literacy Framework Lessons* have endeavoured to incorporate all of the above with one exception, the teaching of phonics. The Government is advising that phonics is taught using a systematic, discrete and time-limited programme. However, where possible we have made links to phonic focuses that you might want to identify when teaching the lesson.

It is important to note that the renewed Framework is advocating a change from the Searchlight model of teaching early reading to the 'simple view of reading', *"The knowledge and skills within the four Searchlight strategies are subsumed within the two dimensions of word recognition and language comprehension of the 'two simple views of reading'. For beginner readers, priority should be given to securing word recognition, knowledge and skills"* (from the PNS Core Papers document). Phonic work will be time limited and as children develop their early reading skills they will then move from learning to read to learning to learn.

Using the book

The book is divided into three parts, called Blocks: Narrative Block, Non-fiction Block and Poetry Block. This reflects the structure of the renewed Framework planning. The Blocks are divided into Units, each Unit covers a different text-type within the Block, for example in the Narrative Block there might be one Unit which covers 'myths and legends' and another that covers 'plays'. Units are taught on a specified amount of weeks and are split into Phases. Phases vary in length and are essentially a way to focus on a specific part of teaching relating to the Unit. Phases are then divided into days, or lessons, which then contain the teaching activities. Unlike the *100 All New Literacy Hours,* this book has not been divided into terms because one of the main points of the Framework is flexibility and this structure will let teachers adapt to their particular children's needs.

Block [genres] ➤ Units [text-type] ➤ Phases [section of Unit] ➤ Days/Lessons [Individual lessons]

Units

Each Unit covers a different text-type, or genre and because of this each Unit has its own introduction containing the following:

Objectives: All objectives for the Unit are listed under their strand names.

Progression: Statements about the progression that the children should make within the Unit's focus, for example narrative text-type.

Aspects of learning: Key aspects of learning that the Unit covers.

Prior learning: Key elements that the children need to be able to do before they commence the lessons.

Cross-curricular opportunities: Integrating other areas of the curriculum into the literacy lessons.

Resources: Everything required for the lesson that teachers may not have readily available.

Teaching sequence: This is an overview chart of the Unit. It shows the number of Phases, children's objectives, a summary of activities and the learning outcomes.

Unit lesson plans

The lesson plans all follow the same format. There are three columns and each contains different information.

Key features: The key features column provides an at-a-glance view of the key aspects of learning covered in the lesson.

Stages: The stages column provides the main lesson plans.

Additional opportunities: This column provides additional opportunities for the lesson. This is where there will be links made to phonics, high frequency words, support or extension activities and any other relevant learning opportunities.

End of Phase

At the end of each Phase there are three boxes containing Guided reading or writing ideas, Assessment ideas and Further work.

Guided: The guided box contains ideas for guided reading or writing. These have been included separately as there seems to be a trend to do this work outside of the literacy hour lesson. These ideas can either be integrated into a lesson or taught at a separate time.

Assessment: There are two types of assessment.

End of Phase assessments: These are mainly observations of the children or simple tasks to see whether they have understood what has been taught in the Phase. Teachers are referred back to the learning outcomes in the teaching sequence in the Unit introduction.

End of Unit assessments: These are activities which range from interactive activities, to working from a stimulus image, to completing a photocopiable sheet. They can be found on the CD-ROM accompanying this series.

Further work: Further work provides opportunities for the teacher to extend or support the children following the assessment activity.

Photocopiable pages

At the end of each Unit are the photocopiable pages. These can also be found on the CD-ROM.

Using the CD-ROM

This is a basic guide for using the CD-ROM; for more detailed information please go to 'How to use the CD-ROM' on the start-up screen of the CD-ROM.

The CD-ROM contains resources for each book in the series. These might include: text extracts, differentiated text extracts, editable text extracts, photocopiable pages, interactive activities, images, videos, audio files, PowerPoint files, weblinks and assessment activities. There are also skeleton frames based on Sue Palmer's skeletons for teaching non-fiction text types. Also on the CD-ROM are the lesson notes for easy planning as Word file documents.

You can access resources in a number of ways:

Phase menu: The Phase menu provides all the resources used in that Phase. There are tabs at the top of the page denoting the resource type, for example 'Text'. If you click on this tab you will see a series of buttons to your left; if you press these then you will be taken to the other texts used within that Phase. You can print two versions of the text: either the screen – which shows any annotations made (see Whiteboard tools below) or Print PDF version, which will print an A4 size.

Resources menu: The resource menu lists every resource that is available on the CD-ROM. You can search by type of resource.

Whiteboard tools: This series contains a set of whiteboard tools. These can be used with any interactive whiteboard and from a computer connected to a projector. The tools available are: Hand tool – so that when you zoom in you can move around the screen; Zoom in; Zoom out; Pen tool for freehand writing or drawing; Highlighter; Line tool; Box tool; Text tool; Eraser tool; Clear screen; Hide annotations; Colour. You cannot save any changes made to the texts so always remember to 'Print Screen' when you annotate the CD-ROM pages.

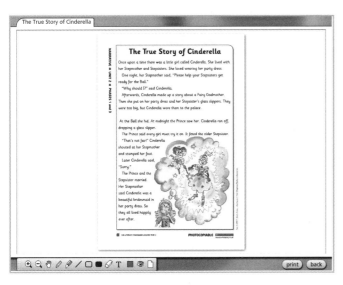

Speak and listen for a range of purposes on paper and on screen strand checklist

	Narrative Unit 1	Narrative Unit 2	Narrative Unit 3	Narrative Unit 4	Non-fiction Unit 1	Non-fiction Unit 2	Non-fiction Unit 3	Non-fiction Unit 4	Poetry Unit 1	Poetry Unit 2	Poetry Unit 3
Strand 1 Speaking											
Speak with clarity and use appropriate intonation when reading and reciting texts.					✔				✔	✔	✔
Tell real and imagined stories using the conventions of familiar story language.	✔	✔									
Explain ideas and processes using imaginative and adventurous vocabulary and non-verbal gestures to support communication.						✔	✔	✔			
Strand 2 Listening and responding											
Listen to others in class, ask relevant questions and follow instructions.			✔		✔	✔	✔				
Listen to talk by an adult, remember some specific points and identify what they have learned.						✔					
Respond to presentations by describing characters, repeating some highlights and commenting constructively.	✔	✔		✔					✔	✔	✔
Strand 3 Group discussion and interaction											
Ensure everyone contributes, allocate tasks, and consider alternatives and reach agreement.					✔	✔			✔	✔	✔
Work effectively in groups by ensuring that each group member takes a turn challenging, supporting and moving on.			✔						✔	✔	✔
Listen to each other's views and preferences, agree the next steps to take and identify contributions by each group member.								✔	✔	✔	✔
Strand 4 Drama											
Adopt appropriate roles in small or large groups and consider alternative courses of action.			✔								
Present part of traditional stories, own stories or work from different parts of the curriculum for members of their own class.	✔	✔		✔							
Consider how mood or atmosphere are created in live or recorded performance.									✔	✔	✔

Read for a range of purposes on paper and on screen strand checklist

	Narrative Unit 1	Narrative Unit 2	Narrative Unit 3	Narrative Unit 4	Non-fiction Unit 1	Non-fiction Unit 2	Non-fiction Unit 3	Non-fiction Unit 4	Poetry Unit 1	Poetry Unit 2	Poetry Unit 3
Strand 5 Word recognition											
Read independently and with increasing fluency longer and less familiar texts.	✔	✔	✔	✔	✔	✔	✔	✔	✔	✔	✔
Spell with increasing accuracy and confidence, drawing on word recognition and knowledge of word structure and spelling patterns.			✔	✔	✔			✔	✔	✔	✔
Know how to tackle unfamiliar words which are not completely decodable.			✔	✔	✔			✔	✔	✔	✔
Read and spell less common alternative graphemes including trigraphs.			✔	✔	✔			✔	✔	✔	✔
Read high and medium frequency words independently and automatically.	✔	✔	✔	✔	✔	✔	✔	✔	✔	✔	✔
Strand 6 Word structure and spelling											
Spell with increasing accuracy and confidence, drawing on word recognition and knowledge of word structure, and spelling patterns including common inflections and use of double letters.	✔	✔	✔	✔	✔	✔	✔	✔	✔	✔	✔
Read and spell less common alternative graphemes including trigraphs.	✔	✔	✔	✔	✔	✔	✔	✔	✔	✔	✔
Strand 7 Understanding and interpreting texts											
Draw together ideas and information from across a whole text, using simple signposts in the text.	✔	✔			✔		✔	✔			
Give some reasons why things happen or characters change.	✔	✔		✔		✔					
Explain organisational features of texts, including alphabetical order, layout, diagrams, captions, hyperlinks and bullet points.					✔	✔	✔	✔			
Use syntax and context to build their store of vocabulary when reading for meaning.											
Explore how particular words are used, including words and expressions with similar meanings.						✔			✔	✔	✔
Strand 8 Engaging with and responding to texts											
Read whole books on their own, choosing and justifying selections.											
Engage with books through exploring and enacting interpretations.	✔		✔	✔	✔	✔					
Explain their reactions to texts, commenting on important aspects.	✔		✔					✔	✔		✔

Write for a range of purposes on paper and on screen strand checklist

	Narrative Unit 1	Narrative Unit 2	Narrative Unit 3	Narrative Unit 4	Non-fiction Unit 1	Non-fiction Unit 2	Non-fiction Unit 3	Non-fiction Unit 4	Poetry Unit 1	Poetry Unit 2	Poetry Unit 3
Strand 9 Creating and shaping texts											
Draw on knowledge and experience of texts in deciding and planning what and how to write.	✔	✔			✔	✔	✔		✔	✔	✔
Sustain form in narrative, including use of person and time.			✔	✔							
Maintain consistency in non-narrative, including purpose and tense.					✔						
Make adventurous word and language choices appropriate to style and purpose of text.							✔		✔	✔	✔
Select from different presentational features to suit particular writing purposes on paper and on screen.	✔	✔		✔	✔	✔	✔	✔	✔	✔	✔
Strand 10 Text structure and organisation											
Use planning to establish clear sections for writing.	✔	✔	✔			✔	✔	✔			
Use appropriate language to make sections hang together.	✔			✔	✔	✔	✔	✔			
Strand 11 Sentence structure and punctuation											
Write simple and compound sentences and begin to use subordination in relation to time and reason.	✔	✔				✔	✔				
Compose sentences using tense consistently (present and past).			✔	✔			✔				
Use question marks and use commas to separate items in a list.							✔				
Strand 12 Presentation											
Write legibly, using upper and lower case letters appropriately within words, and observing correct spacing within and between words.									✔	✔	✔
Form and use the basic handwriting joins.									✔	✔	✔
Word-process short narrative and non-narrative texts.		✔		✔			✔	✔	✔	✔	✔

NARRATIVE
UNIT 1 Stories with familiar settings

Speak and listen for a range of purposes on paper and on screen

Strand 1 Speaking
- Tell real and imagined stories using the conventions of familiar story language.

Strand 2 Listening and responding
- Respond to presentations by describing characters, repeating some highlights and commenting constructively.

Strand 4 Drama
- Present part of traditional stories, own stories or work from different parts of the curriculum for members of their own class.

Read for a range of purposes on paper and on screen

Strand 5 Word recognition: decoding (reading) and encoding (spelling)
- Read independently and with increasing fluency longer and less familiar texts.
- Read high and medium frequency words independently and automatically.

Strand 6 Word structure and spelling
- Spell with increasing accuracy and confidence, drawing on word recognition and knowledge of word structure and spelling patterns including common inflections and use of double letters.
- Read and spell less common alternative graphemes including trigraphs.

Strand 7 Understanding and interpreting texts
- Draw together ideas and information from across a whole text, using simple signposts in the text.
- Give some reasons why things happen and/or characters change.

Strand 8 Engaging with and responding to texts
- Engage with books through exploring and enacting interpretations.
- Explain their reactions to texts, commenting on important aspects.

Write for a range of purposes on paper and on screen

Strand 9 Creating and shaping texts
- Draw on knowledge and experience of texts in deciding and planning what and how to write.
- Select from different presentational features to suit particular writing purposes on paper and on screen.

Strand 10 Text structure and organisation
- Use planning to establish clear sections for writing.
- Use appropriate language to make sections hang together.

Strand 11 Sentence structure and punctuation
- Write simple and compound sentences and begin to use subordination in relation to time and reason.

Progression in narrative

In this year, children are moving towards:
- Identifying the sequence: opening – something happens – events to sort it out – ending; identifying temporal connectives and talking about how they signal the passing of time; making deductions about why events take place in a particular order by looking at characters' actions and their consequences.
- Understanding that we know what characters are like from what they do and say as well as how they behave; predicting how they might behave.

UNIT 1 ◄ Stories with familiar settings *continued*

■ Retelling familiar stories using narrative structure and dialogue from the text.

Key aspects of learning covered in this Unit

Problem solving
Children will respond to a task using trial and error and consider a range of possible solutions.

Creative thinking
Children will generate imaginative ideas to make connections and see relationships between different modes of communication.
Children will experiment with different modes of communication to respond to different points of view.

Evaluation
Children will discuss success criteria for their written and oral work, give feedback to others and judge the effectiveness of their own writing and speaking.

Social skills
When working collaboratively children will learn about listening to and respecting other people's ideas and taking on different roles within a group.

Communication
Children will recognise communication in different modes. They will work collaboratively to discuss, plan and create a story.

Prior learning

Before starting this Unit check that the children can:
■ Listen to and tell a story; recognise that has a story has different parts.
■ Identify story elements: characters, setting and key events; sequence the events of a story; make reference to characters and their viewpoints.
■ Work collaboratively in a group, taking turns and reaching agreement.
■ Plan a story; write simple and compound sentences, and use connectives.
■ Use the third person and past tense consistently in narrative writing.
If they need further support please refer to prior Unit or a similar Unit in Year 1.

Resources

Sequence 1, Phase 1:
Going Shopping by Eileen Jones ❖; Photocopiable page 26 'Storyboard'
Sequence 1, Phase 2:
In a Crowded Playground by Eileen Jones ❖
Sequence 1, Phase 3:
In a Crowded Playground by Eileen Jones ❖; *Going Shopping* by Eileen Jones ❖; *Story planner: Going Shopping* by Eileen Jones ❖; Photocopiable page 27 'Character storyline'; Photocopiable page 28 'Alarm'; Photocopiable page 29 'Story planner'; 'Alarm' interactive activity ❖
Sequence 2, Phase 1:
Holiday Time by Eileen Jones ❖; *Going Shopping* by Eileen Jones ❖; *In a Crowded Playground* by Eileen Jones ❖; Photocopiable page 26 'Storyboard'
Sequence 2, Phase 2:
Photocopiable page 29 'Story planner'; Completed version of photocopiable page 26 'Storyboard' (see page 21 for details)
Sequence 2, Phase 3:
Photocopiable page 30 'Reading a story'; Assessment activity 'How to plan a story' ❖

Cross-curricular opportunities

PSHE – Developing good relationships

UNIT 1 ■ Teaching Sequence 1

Phase	Children's objectives	Summary of activities	Learning outcomes
1	I can sequence the main parts of a story.	Listen to a story and draw main events. Use pictures to tell and sequence a story. Draw, sequence and tell a new story.	Children can sequence the different parts of a story.
2	I can understand that different story characters have different points of view.	Role play a character; tell the story from that character's point of view. Explore different courses of action for characters.	Children can understand that characters have different points of view and could follow different courses of action.
3	I can show a character's storyline in pictures. I can identify sections of a story. I can identify temporal connectives.	Investigate the order of character action in a story. Identify sections of a story; learn how to represent content in note form. Recognise and use temporal connectives.	Children can describe what a character does in a story. Children can understand story structure and the use of temporal connectives.

UNIT 1 ■ Teaching Sequence 2

Phase	Children's objectives	Summary of activities	Learning outcomes
1	I can make predictions about what story characters might do. I can plan a story in pictures. I can plan a character storyline in pictures.	Predict character action and story progression from a story opening. Plan and sequence a story pictorially. Analyse character actions in a planned story.	Children can plan and sequence pictorially a story.
2	I can write story planning notes.	Collaborate on class planning notes. Write own story planning notes.	Children can use the *opening – something happens – events to sort it out – ending* structure to plan a story.
3	I can use notes to write a story. I can use time connectives in a story.	Collaborate on using notes to write a story. Collaborate on using time connectives within a story. Use notes to write a story. Read and evaluate another child's story.	Children can write notes and use them to write a story.

Provide copies of the objectives for the children.

DAY 1 ■ Listen to the story

Key features	Stages	Additional opportunities
	Introduction Print a copy of *Going Shopping* from the CD-ROM. Explain to the children that you are going to read a story aloud to them. Every so often you will pause and they will draw what has happened at each stage in the story. Give every child a copy of photocopiable page 26 'Storyboard' for them to use for their drawings.	**Phonics:** goods, brown **HFW:** sister, new, as, little
Communication: recognise communication in different modes	**Independent work** Discuss what the children must do. What skills will be most important? Agree on the need for careful listening. Share ideas on how to be a good listener. Children should be: looking at you; watching your face and gestures; hearing changes in your voice to help them understand what is happening in the story. Read the story, pausing in four places – after *...they set off; ...he had turned; ...Neesha's hat!;* and *...look after you.* At each pause, allow the children time to think before they do their drawings.	**Support:** children work in pairs
	Plenary Ask the children what the story was about. Let some children display their pictures. Does everyone seem to agree? Did some people hear more?	

DAY 2 ■ Storytellers

Key features	Stages	Additional opportunities
	Introduction Before the lesson, invent a simple story with a familiar setting. Follow the pattern of *opening – something happens – events to sort it out – ending.* Create four pictures of the new story, set out in the style of photocopiable page 26 'Storyboard' that the children used yesterday. Do not show the pictures to the children.	**Phonics:** goods, brown **HFW:** sister, new, as, little
Communication: recognise communication in different modes	**Speaking and listening** Explain to the class that it is story time again! This time you going to be a storyteller rather than a story reader. Tell the children your story, using the pictures as a guide to occasionally glance at. Use your voice to signal changes in focus, to emphasise key words, and to adopt expressive tone and gestures. Remind the children of the pictures that they drew yesterday.	
Social skills: listen to and respect other people's ideas	**Independent work** Put the children into pairs or threes. Each child should have a turn as storyteller, using their pictures from yesterday to tell the *Going Shopping* story to the other(s). Remind the storytellers to keep their listeners' attention using their voice and face – listeners should keep their eyes on the face of their storyteller.	**Support:** children share storytelling with a partner
	Plenary Ask: *How well did you listen? What helped to keep your interest in the story?*	

DAY 3 ▪ What happens next?

Key features	Stages	Additional opportunities
	Introduction Display the *Going Shopping* story from the CD-ROM and read it aloud.	**Phonics:** g*oo*ds, br*ow*n **HFW:** sister, new, as, little
Evaluation: judge the effectiveness of their own writing	**Speaking and listening** Let partners discuss the story and their picture storyboards from Day 1. Is there more detail than they noticed as listeners? What did they leave out of their pictures? Share ideas. Do the children think it is easier to remember stories if you just listen? Suggest that Mum, Dwayne and Neesha have now left the supermarket. Ask: *Where could they be?* Share ideas on familiar settings – park, home, another shop and so on. Ask: *What will happen? How will the new story end?*	
Creative thinking: generate imaginative ideas	**Independent work** Let the children create four new pictures about Mum, Dwayne and Neesha on photocopiable page 26 'Storyboard'. Remind them that something should happen and the story needs to come to an ending.	**Support:** children may want to rehearse ideas with an adult or partner
Social skills: work collaboratively	**Plenary** Ask the children to display their storyboards. Let everyone use their pictures to tell their story to a partner. Encourage them to use the past tense.	

Guided reading
Give the children copies of *Going Shopping* and read it with them in groups. Help them to discuss what happens in the story. Ask them to think about the different parts of the story. Is one part more important than the others? Are all the parts needed?

Assessment
Invite the children to retell the story *Going Shopping* to a partner.
Now ask them to repeat the exercise, taking turns with their partner to retell part of the story, being careful to put events in the correct sequence. Encourage them to use the past tense. Can the children sustain its use? Refer back to the learning outcomes on page 11.

Further work
Suggest that the children continue to be storytellers, but this time they can tell a story of their own to a partner.
They must be careful to sequence the events of their story correctly and to use the past tense.
A pictorial plan of their story could be helpful.

DAY 1 ▪ Story characters

Key features	Stages	Additional opportunities
	### Introduction Display and read aloud *In a Crowded Playground* from the CD-ROM. Make sure that everyone has understood the story. Introduce the word 'character'. Ask: *What does it mean? Who are the two main characters here? Are there others?* (Dad, other children.)	**Phonics:** g*oo*d, pl*ay*, n*ew* **HFW:** out, home, time, good
Problem solving: consider a range of possible solutions	### Speaking and listening Working in pairs, ask the children to focus on Jack, and discuss his side of the story. Encourage them to mention events in the correct sequence. Share the results, and then invite the children to repeat the process for Chloe.	
Social skills: work collaboratively	### Independent work Now ask pairs of children to use role play to re-enact the story – one child takes the part of Jack and the other is Chloe. They need to retain the story's events and sequence, but not necessarily the precise dialogue. Improvised dialogue works well. Afterwards, encourage the children to think about what has happened to their character, and then prepare to retell the story from their character's point of view. Encourage oral rehearsal, reminding the children to use 'I', and not their character's name.	
	### Plenary Invite several Jacks and Chloes to retell their story to the rest of the class. Ask: *Do we now know more about these characters? Why?*	

DAY 2 ▪ Same scene, different setting

Key features	Stages	Additional opportunities
	### Introduction Talk about the children's role-play activities from yesterday. Display *In a Crowded Playground* from the CD-ROM and read it together.	**Phonics:** g*oo*d, pl*ay*, n*ew* **HFW:** out, home, time, good, new
Creative thinking: generate imaginative ideas	### Speaking and listening Let partners remind each other of the story's events and their sequence. What did Jack do? What actions did Chloe take? Suggest that the writer could have used this same playground setting, but created a different story by making the characters take different courses of action. Share some possibilities. (For example: Jack approaches someone; Chloe sees Jack but does not help; Jack goes home unhappy; Chloe apologises.)	
Problem solving: consider a range of possible solutions	### Independent work Working in pairs, ask the children to plan a new course of action for the characters. They can then use role play – with one child as Jack and the other as Chloe – to enact the new story. Afterwards, encourage the children to think about what has happened to their character and to retell this new story from his or her point of view.	
Social skills: work collaboratively	### Plenary Ask the pairs of children to come together into groups of four so that each pair of children can retell their story to a new audience.	

Guided reading

Give the children copies of *In a Crowded Playground* and read it with them in groups. Help them to discuss what happened in the story.

Ask them to think about the characters in the story. How would they describe each character?

Assessment

Focus on the main characters in the story. Ask: *Which one interests you most? Why? What is that character's point of view?*

Assess how well the children can retell part of the story from one character's point of view.

Refer back to the learning outcomes on page 11.

Further work

Expand the assessment work to include minor characters. Let the children describe what some of them did in the story. Can they suggest a new course of action for one of the minor characters?

DAY 1 ◼ Pictorial storylines

Key features	Stages	Additional opportunities
	Introduction Display *In a Crowded Playground* from the CD-ROM and read it together.	**Phonics:** good, play, new **HFW:** out, home, time, good
	Speaking and listening Suggest to the children that they each tell their partner one thing that either Jack or Chloe did in the story. Share some results as a class, writing one or two important examples on the board.	
Communication: see relationships between different modes of communication	**Independent work** Give out copies of photocopiable page 27 'Character storyline'. Ask the children to choose either Jack or Chloe – perhaps the one whose role they took yesterday. They need to think about what that character did in the story. Ask: *Are you thinking of their actions in the correct order?* Having entered the character's name at the top of the photocopiable sheet, they can draw pictures to depict the character's storyline. They should keep to a pictorial story only.	**Support:** children work on their own photocopiable page, but collaborate with a partner **Extend:** children complete two photocopiable pages, one for each character
	Plenary Let children present their storylines, explaining what the character is doing at each stage. Save the children's work.	

DAY 2 ◼ Character actions 2

Key features	Stages	Additional opportunities
	Introduction Remind the children about yesterday's work. Suggest that a writer might draw a character's storyline. Discuss why this might be. (To check the order of the character's actions made sense.) Emphasise the importance of story events being in an order that makes sense. Point out that one event usually leads to another.	**Phonics:** good, play, new **HFW:** out, home, time, good
Problem solving: consider a range of possible solutions	**Independent work** Give out copies of photocopiable page 28 'Alarm'. The children must cut out the pictures and put them in the correct order. Let them stick the pictures on to a piece of paper when they are happy that their chosen sequence tells a story that makes sense.	**Support:** children work on their own photocopiable page, but collaborate with a partner
Communication: work collaboratively to plan a story	**Plenary** Display the 'Alarm' interactive activity from the CD-ROM. Let the children present their answers. Which sequence makes most sense? Emphasise how, with the correct sequence, one event leads to another.	**Extend:** children do writing for both characters

DAY 3 ▮ Story structure

Key features	Stages	Additional opportunities
	Introduction Display *Going Shopping* from the CD-ROM and read the story together.	**Phonics:** goods, brown **HFW:** sister, new, as, little
Problem solving: consider a range of possible solutions **Communication:** recognise communication in different modes	**Independent work** Remind the children of your first reading on Phase 1, Day 1. Ask the children to discuss with their partners what you did, how many times you paused for them to draw, and where in the text you paused. Compare answers as a class. Confirm the four places where you paused. Divide up the text so the divisions are clear. What part of the story is each section? Write the labels *opening; something happens; events to sort it out; ending.* Keep moving between partner and class discussion as you model notes on the content of each section. Encourage the children to contribute. Demonstrate writing words and phrases, not sentences. Would bullet points be a clear form of presentation? Show the children *Story planner: Going Shopping* from the CD-ROM.	
	Plenary Discuss the story planner. Compare the notes with the story text. Ask the children which they think the writer started with – the completed story or the planning notes? Save the notes you have made.	

DAY 4 ▮ Using time connectives

Key features	Stages	Additional opportunities
	Introduction Display *Going Shopping* from the CD-ROM and read it together.	**Phonics:** while, mean, soon **HFW:** next, now
Communication: work collaboratively to discuss a story **Problem solving:** consider a range of possible solutions	**Speaking and listening** Investigate the order of events in the story with the children. Suggest that an event in one part may lead to an event in a later section. Encourage the children to work with a partner to find an example. Share ideas as a class, identifying some in the text. (For example, Neesha needing her spotty hat leads to Dwayne finding Neesha and Mum in the supermarket.) Suggest that the writer can help the reader to follow a time sequence by using time connectives. Highlight *Later.* What does this time connective tell the reader? Use partner then class discussion to help the children identify other time connectives – *first, next, soon, just then, now* – in answer to questions. For example: *Which word tells us Mum and Dwayne start to shop? Which phrase near the end moves the story on in time?*	
	Independent work Give out copies of *In a Crowded Playground* from the CD-ROM for partners to re-read a section at a time. Give clues to help them find temporal connectives: *then, meanwhile, just then, after that, first, next, later, now.*	**Extend:** children suggest alternative time connectives
	Plenary Make a class list of other possible time connectives.	

DAY 5 ■ Analysing the structure

Key features	Stages	Additional opportunities
	### Introduction Display *In a Crowded Playground* from the CD-ROM and read it together. Explain that you want to read it in four parts (as you did on Day 1, Phase 1).	**Phonics:** g*oo*d, pl*ay*, n*ew* **HFW:** out, home, time, good
	### Speaking and listening Let children discuss with their partners where you should make your pauses. Share some ideas as a class and divide up the text into *opening; something happens; events to sort it out; ending.* Remind the children about the notes you made on Phase 3, Day 3, about the content of each section of *Going Shopping.* Discuss possible notes that you could make about the opening of *In a Crowded Playground.*	
Creative thinking: generate imaginative ideas to make connections	### Independent work Give out photocopiable page 29 'Story planner' and copies of *In a Crowded Playground.* Ask the children, working individually or with a partner, to make brief notes on the content of each section.	**Support:** children work with a partner
Evaluation: judge the effectiveness of their own writing	### Plenary Invite children to read out their notes. Do they represent the story structure well? Work together on a class version.	

Guided reading
Give groups time to read and compare *Going Shopping* and *In a Crowded Playground.* Ask your teaching assistant to discuss with them how the two stories progress. Which are the important events in both stories? Are the stories created in a similar way?

Assessment
Focus on the structure of the two stories. Can the children identify the different sections of one of the stories? Can the children identify the same sections in the other story? Refer back to the learning outcomes on page 11.

Further work
Expand the assessment work to include minor characters. Let the children describe what some of them did in the story. Can they suggest a new course of action for one of the minor characters?

DAY 1 ■ Holiday time

Key features	Stages	Additional opportunities
	Introduction Tell the children that you are going to read them a new story today. Display and read *Holiday Time* from the CD-ROM. Cover the illustration to begin with.	**Phonics:** c*are*, wh*ole*, sh*out* **HFW:** your, got, two
Problem solving: consider a range of possible solutions	**Speaking and listening** Allow time for the children to discuss the story with their partners before you share answers to questions such as: *Where is the story set? Who are the characters? Which character do we know most about? Which one least? Does the story seem complete?* Explain that the story they have heard is only the first part of the story. Encourage partner discussion of ideas on how the story may progress. Share some ideas as a class.	
Communication: work collaboratively to discuss, plan and create a story	**Independent work** Put the children into groups of four. Suggest they use discussion and then role play to predict the character's actions and the progression of the story. Encourage the groups to try out more than one idea.	
	Plenary Let the groups enact their dramas for the rest of the class.	

DAY 2 ■ A story in pictures

Key features	Stages	Additional opportunities
	Introduction Ask the children: *What are the four sections of a story?* Write on the board – *opening; something happens; events to sort it out; ending.* Display and read the *Holiday Time* story beginning from the CD-ROM. Ask: *Does it contain all four sections?* Remind the children of the dramas they created yesterday.	**Phonics:** c*are*, wh*ole*, sh*out*, s*ort*, *out* **HFW:** your, got, two
Communication: work collaboratively to discuss, plan and create a story	**Speaking and listening** Suggest that the children may now have new ideas of their own about what the characters will do and how this story will continue. Let them discuss ideas with their partner and then try them out in role play. The children need to ask themselves: *Will my ideas form a complete story? Will there be the four sections needed?*	
	Independent work Give out copies of photocopiable page 26 'Storyboard'. Ask the children to record their ideas in a pictorial plan, drawing a picture for each section of their story idea.	
Evaluation: give feedback to others	**Plenary** Let the children become storytellers, using their pictorial storyboards for support. Suggest that the listeners provide oral feedback. Was there something in the story they did not understand? The storytellers may want to make changes to a picture. Save the storyboards.	

DAY 3 ◼ Building up characters

Key features	Stages	Additional opportunities
	Introduction Return to the children's pictorial storyboards. Discuss the importance of the characters and what they do. Talk about the characters' actions in the stories you read in Sequence 1 of this Unit.	**Phonics:** purse, were **HFW:** brother, there
Creative thinking: generate imaginative ideas	**Speaking and listening** Ask the children to tell their partners about an important character in their planned story. What do they do? What sequence are their actions in? Display one of the children's completed character pictorial storylines from Sequence 1, Phase 3, Day 1.	
	Independent work Suggest the children choose a main character from the story they invented yesterday and draw pictures showing the sequence of the actions that this character will take. Invite the children to look at their completed character lines. Do the actions make sense? Encourage them to ask their partners for advice.	**Support:** children list the character's actions orally (to a partner or adult) before they draw **Extend:** children complete the storyline of a second character
Evaluation: give feedback to others	**Plenary** Let children talk about their characters. Do they sound interesting? Do the other children look forward to reading about them in a story?	

Guided reading
Ask the children to read and compare *Going Shopping* and *In a Crowded Playground* from the CD-ROM with your teaching assistant. This time, they should concentrate on the characters in the story. Do they think any of the characters are similar? What character actions are similar?

Assessment
Challenge the children to tell their partner the beginning of a story. Suggest that the story should be set in a school and that the two main characters in the story should be introduced. Can their partner predict what one of the characters will do? Refer back to the learning outcomes on page 11.

Further work
Following on from the assessment activity, ask the children to remind themselves of how the character behaved in the *Holiday Time* story beginning they heard.
Can they predict the behaviour of both main characters throughout the story?

DAY 1 ▪ Planning a story

Key features	Stages	Additional opportunities
	Introduction Display photocopiable page 29 'Story planner'. Remind the children of what the planner is used for – to write notes before beginning to write a story. Have ready a completed pictorial storyboard showing a brand new story (not linked to *Holiday Time*). Explain to the class that you have already planned this new story in pictures – now you need to make written notes. Show the children your storyboard. Speaking as a storyteller, recount what is happening in the first picture. Make sure that you mention the setting and some characters.	**Phonics:** note, sort, out **HFW:** out, some
Communication: work collaboratively to discuss and plan a story	**Speaking and listening** Let the children discuss with a partner what your notes should be for the *opening* section of your story. Come together as a class and share ideas. Then demonstrate making notes for the *opening* section. Progress through the pictures, telling each section of the story before asking for help with the notes. Move between partner and class discussion as you model using the story planner to make notes on each section. Demonstrate writing words and phrases, not sentences.	
	Plenary Discuss and save the completed notes. Emphasise that although you have written notes, they contain enough detail for you to understand them later.	

DAY 2 ▪ Making notes

Key features	Stages	Additional opportunities
	Introduction Display and read out the notes you made yesterday. Investigate their form and features. Ask the children: *What is the purpose of the notes? Will they be useful when I start writing my story?* Agree that although brief, their meaning is still clear to you and you will be able to work from them later. Compare the notes with your pictorial storyboard, reminding the children how you wrote the notes.	**Phonics:** note, sort, out **HFW:** out, some
	Speaking and listening Return to the children's pictorial storyboards from Sequence 2, Phase 1. Suggest that children remind themselves of the content of their stories by telling them to their partners.	
Creative thinking: generate imaginative ideas to make connections	**Independent work** Give out copies of photocopiable page 29 'Story planner'. Let the children complete the sheet with notes on their story. Emphasise that they should keep the notes brief, but include enough information to help them when they write their story text.	**Support:** children write only one or two notes for each section
Evaluation: judge the effectiveness of their own writing	**Plenary** Let children present their notes. Do the stories sound as if they will be exciting?	

Guided reading

Read a familiar short story together. Help groups of children to discuss how one part of the story fits well with the other sections.

Assessment

Assess the children's recognition of the different sections of a story. Ask, about one story: *How did the writer plan the story? Did she write sentences in her planning? How did a plan help the writer?* Refer back to the learning outcomes on page 11.

Further work

Ask the children to pretend to be the writer of the story. They want to change the final section of the story. How can they give the story a different ending? Do the other sections still make sense?

DAY 1 ■ Modelling story writing

Key features	Stages	Additional opportunities
	Introduction Display the pictorial storyboard you created earlier (see Sequence 2, Phase 2, Day 1) and remind the children that this is a plan for the story you intend to write. Ask them what else they think will help. Display the story planner you created together. Ask: *Can we still understand the notes?* Demonstrate using the notes for the *opening* to help you write the beginning of your story. Encourage the children to make suggestions as you model how to construct complete sentences.	**Phonics:** note, sort, out **HFW:** out, some
Social skills: listen to and respect other people's ideas		
	Speaking and listening Progress through the notes, moving between partner and class discussion as you model the writing of the next two sections. Use a few temporal connectives, but deliberately leave them out of much of the text.	
Creative thinking: generate imaginative ideas to make connections	**Independent work** Ask the children, working individually or with partners, to write the final section, the *ending*, for you. **Plenary** Listen to and look at some of the writing. Which one would you like as your story ending? Add an ending to your story and save the complete text.	**Support:** children have adult support and sentence starters

DAY 2 ■ Revising time connectives

Key features	Stages	Additional opportunities
	Introduction Revise temporal connectives from Sequence 1, Phase 3. Ask the children: *What is a time connective? Can you think of an example?* Compile and save a class collection of time connectives. Display and read aloud your completed story from yesterday.	**Phonics:** time, later **HFW:** next, now
	Speaking and listening Ask the children to work with a partner to find a time connective, but limit the area of their search (perhaps to within a certain paragraph). Share results as a class.	
Problem solving: consider a range of possible solutions	**Independent work** Print copies of your story and ask the children, perhaps working with partners, to circle the time connectives. Suggest that your story needs more time connectives. Let the children put a mark where the addition of one would improve the text. What time connectives would they use? The children could use a colour or number code and then write a key with their suggested words or phrases.	**Support:** children work with a partner on only part of the story
	Plenary Share ideas. Have children often made the same choice? Agree on and add ones that most help to make the story's time sequence clear.	

DAY 3 ■ Beginning to write

Key features	Stages	Additional opportunities
	Introduction Tell the children that your story is written – now it's time for them to have a go! Remind them of the stages of your work: a pictorial storyboard; creating a story planner; writing the story text.	**Phonics:** note, sort, out **HFW:** out, some
Social skills: work collaboratively	**Speaking and listening** Return to the children's pictorial storyboards and story planner (see Sequence 2, Phases 1 and 2) and encourage them to remind themselves of their ideas. Talking their plans through with a partner will help.	
Creative thinking: generate imaginative ideas	**Independent work** Let the children begin writing their stories. Emphasise the benefits of following this sequence as they construct a sentence: ■ rehearsing words mentally; ■ writing the sentence. Remind the children about time connectives and have the class list on display.	**Support:** children write one or two sentences for each section **Extend:** children are encouraged to write longer sections
	Plenary Discuss progress. Listen to some story beginnings. Do the settings vary? What about the characters?	

DAY 4 ■ Completing the stories

Key features	Stages	Additional opportunities
	Introduction Return to yesterday's work. The children are in the middle of writing their stories. What must they be careful of? (The next part must continue smoothly from what they have already written.) Encourage the children to read through what they have written to remind themselves where they have reached in the notes. Emphasise that their notes are there to help them create the story they want. Remind the children about time connectives and have the class list on display.	**Phonics:** note, sort, out **HFW:** out, some
Creative thinking: generate imaginative ideas	**Independent work** Let the children continue writing their stories. Remind them about rehearsing sentences in their heads before they write them down. Pausing to read their story at regular intervals will help the children to remember to use time connectives.	**Support:** children write one or two sentences for each section **Extend:** children are encouraged to write longer sections
Communication: recognise communication in different modes	**Plenary** Discuss progress. Are the stories finished? How useful were the pictorial storyboards and the story planner? Have they made the stories better?	

DAY 5 ■ Evaluating the finished stories

Key features	Stages	Additional opportunities
	Introduction Allow time for the children to complete their story writing and to add their title. Encourage them to re-read their completed work to check for grammatical sense and accuracy. Have they used whole sentences? Do verbs and nouns/pronouns agree?	**Phonics:** note, sort, out **HFW:** out, some
Evaluation: give feedback to others and judge the effectiveness of their own writing	**Speaking and listening** Put the children into pairs. Ask partners to exchange and read each other's story. What do they like? Which character in the story do they find interesting? Why?	
	Independent work Give out copies of photocopiable page 30 'Reading a story'. Ask everyone to fill it in, writing about another child's story. Suggest the children provide the writer with oral as well as written feedback.	**Support:** children are supported by adult or partner to read the evaluation sheet
	Plenary Discuss what the children have learned from the feedback. How would they make their next story even better? Finish with a change to story-reading session, as writers (the children) read their stories aloud.	

Guided writing

Ask a volunteer to read their story to the class and demonstrate how feedback from the other children could be incorporated to improve it.

Assessment

Give the children copies of the photocopiable assessment activity 'How to plan a story' from the CD-ROM. Consider:
Can the children answer the questions confidently?
Is there an area that they remain uncertain of?
Refer back to the learning outcomes on page 11.

Further work

Let the children put their assessment answers into practice by planning a new story set in a familiar setting.

Storyboard

2	4
1	3

Character storyline

What _____ does

1

2

3

4

Illustration © Nova Developments

Alarm

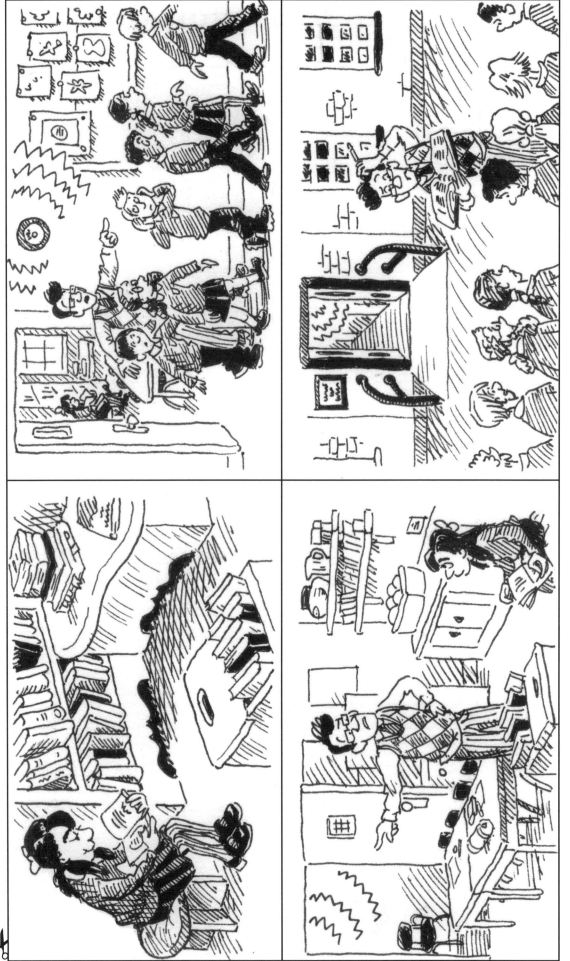

Story planner

Opening

■ ————————————————

————————————————

■ ————————————————

————————————————

■ ————————————————

————————————————

Something happens

■ ————————————————

————————————————

■ ————————————————

————————————————

■ ————————————————

————————————————

Events to sort it out

■ ————————————————

————————————————

■ ————————————————

————————————————

■ ————————————————

————————————————

Ending

■ ————————————————

————————————————

■ ————————————————

————————————————

■ ————————————————

————————————————

Reading a story

Title of the story I read: _____

The writer: _____

What important thing happened in the story? _____

_____

How was it sorted out? _____

_____

How did the story end? _____

_____

What has happened to you like this? _____

_____

NARRATIVE
UNIT 2 Traditional stories

Speak and listen for a range of purposes on paper and on screen

Strand 1 Speaking
- Tell real and imagined stories using the conventions of familiar story language.

Strand 2 Listening and responding
- Respond to presentations by describing characters, repeating some highlights and commenting constructively.

Strand 4 Drama
- Present part of traditional stories, their own stories or work from different parts of the curriculum for members of their own class.

Read for a range of purposes on paper and on screen

Strand 5 Word recognition: knowledge and skills
- Read independently and with increasing fluency longer and less familiar texts.
- Read high and medium frequency words independently and automatically.

Strand 6 Word structure and spelling
- Spell with increasing accuracy and confidence, drawing on word recognition and knowledge of word structure, and spelling patterns including common inflections and use of double letters.
- Read and spell less common alternative graphemes including trigraphs.

Strand 7 Understanding and interpreting texts
- Draw together ideas and information from across a whole text, using simple signposts in the text.
- Give some reasons why things happen and/or characters change.

Write for a range of purposes on paper and on screen

Strand 9 Creating and shaping texts
- Draw on knowledge and experience of texts in deciding and planning what and how to write.
- Select from different presentational features to suit particular writing purposes on paper and on screen.

Strand 10 Text structure and organisation
- Use planning to establish clear sections for writing.

Strand 11 Sentence structure and punctuation
- Write simple and compound sentences and begin to use subordination in relation to time and reason.

Strand 12 Presentation
- Word-process short narrative and non-narrative texts.

Progression in narrative

In this year, children are moving towards:
- Identifying temporal connectives and talking about how they are used to signal the passing of time.
- Understanding that we know what characters are like from what they do and say as well as their appearance; the way the characters speak reflects their personality; the verbs used for dialogue tell us how a character is feeling.

▶

Key aspects of learning covered in this Unit

Problem solving
Children will respond to a task using trial and error and consider a range of possible solutions.

Creative thinking
Children will generate imaginative ideas to make connections and see relationships between different modes of communication.
Children will experiment with different modes of communication to respond to different points of view.

Evaluation
Children will discuss success criteria for their written and oral work, give feedback to others and judge the effectiveness of their own writing and speaking.

Social skills
When working collaboratively children will learn about listening to and respecting other people's ideas and taking on different roles within a group.

Communication
Children will recognise communication in different modes. They will work collaboratively to discuss, plan and create a traditional tale.

Prior learning

Before starting this Unit check that the children can:
■ Recognise speech punctuation.
■ Be familiar with the use of time connectives.
■ Write in complete sentences with capital letters and full stops.
If they need further support please refer to a prior Unit or a similar Unit in Year 1.

Resources

Phase 1:
Cinderella by Eileen Jones ✇; *Cinderella* (differentiated version) by Eileen Jones ✇; *The True Story of Cinderella* by Eileen Jones ✇; *The True Story of Cinderella* (differentiated version) by Eileen Jones ✇; Photocopiable page 47 'What I heard'; Photocopiable page 48 'Cinderella characters'; Photocopiable page 49 'Little Red Riding Hood'; Interactive activity 'Little Red Riding Hood' ✇

Phase 2:
Cinderella by Eileen Jones ✇; *Cinderella* (differentiated version) by Eileen Jones ✇; Photocopiable page 50 'Cinderella's stepmother'; Photocopiable page 26 'Storyboard'

Phase 3:
Cinderella multimodal story by Eileen Jones ✇; *Cinderella* multimodal story (text-only version) by Eileen Jones ✇; *The True Story of Cinderella* by Eileen Jones ✇; Assessment activity 'The True Story of Little Red Riding Hood' ✇

Cross-curricular opportunities

ICT – Writing stories; Creating pictures

UNIT 2 ■ Teaching sequence

Phase	Children's objectives	Summary of activities	Learning outcomes
1	I can use information from a story to describe a character.	Read a traditional story and identify opposing characters. Identify relevant actions by characters. Use hot-seating to portray characters. Add dialogue to a story. Identify, replace and add connectives.	Children can express ideas about a character using evidence from the text
2	I can reverse the roles of 'good' and 'bad' characters and write text to suit the new roles.	Reverse the characteristics of characters in a traditional story. Identify the messages of body language; demonstrate the body language of a 'good' character. Draw a storyboard and write new storylines to suit new character roles. Add connectives to improve text. Write final story.	Children can understand that text must match character action.
3	I can use sound, text and image ideas to portray character.	Read a multimodal story and assess the impact of images and sounds. Revise pictures and sound in a multimodal story to suit the traditional model of the tale.	Children can understand that words, images and sounds can convey different elements of a narrative for a reader. Children can write a traditional narrative using words, sounds and images to convey information about the main characters.

Provide copies of the objectives for the children.

DAY 1 ■ Fairy-tale characters

Key features	Stages	Additional opportunities
	Introduction Tell the children that they are going to read a traditional fairy tale.	**Phonics:** more, wear **HFW:** once, lived
Social skills: work collaboratively	**Speaking and listening** Ask them to share views with a partner about what the story will be like. Is there usually a main character? Will all the characters be similar? Bring the class back together and read the traditional tale *Cinderella* from the CD-ROM. Confirm that a traditional fairy tale usually has a 'good' central character and a villain. Who is the 'good' central character here? Who is the villain?	**Support:** a differentiated version of *Cinderella* is available on the CD-ROM
Problem solving: consider a range of possible solutions	**Independent work** Ask the children to think about Cinderella and the Stepmother. Invite them to list the ways in which Cinderella is a 'good' character, and the ways in which the Stepmother is a villain. The children need to examine what the two characters do and say.	
	Plenary Share ideas. Work together to create a class chart of the general characteristics, actions and speech of the 'good' central character and the villain. Save this for another session.	

DAY 2 ■ Goodies and baddies

Key features	Stages	Additional opportunities
	Introduction Give the children copies of *Cinderella* from the CD-ROM and read the story together. Remind the children about yesterday's work. Question them about Cinderella and use the terms *'good' central character* and *villain*.	**Phonics:** more, wear **HFW:** once, lived
Problem solving: consider a range of possible solutions	**Independent work** Ask the children to work in pairs, one child focusing on Cinderella and the other on the Stepmother. The first child must describe what Cinderella does, using evidence from the text to prove that Cinderella is good. The second child has to do the same for the Stepmother, giving evidence proving that she is a villain. Stress the need to refer to the text. Ask the children to score on their individual whiteboards how convinced they are by what their partner has said. (Scores could be numbers, words or ticks and crosses.)	
	Plenary Ask the class to hold up their scores. Ask some children who gave high scores to explain what it was that they found convincing in their partner's evidence. Ask them: *What evidence in the text is important?*	

DAY 3 ■ In the hot-seat

Key features	Stages	Additional opportunities

Introduction
Display and read *Cinderella* from the CD-ROM.
Remind the children of the previous day's partner discussion.
Introduce and explain the term 'hot-seating'. Demonstrate the technique by taking the hot-seat as the Fairy Godmother and answering questions from your teaching assistant. Emphasise that you are answering as if you were the Fairy Godmother, not yourself. Try to use words from the text.

Phonics: *more, wear*
HFW: do, ball

Speaking and listening
Creative thinking: generate imaginative ideas

Ask the children to work with a partner. Each must take a role – Cinderella or the Stepmother – and take a turn in the hot-seat as the other person questions them about what they said and did in the story.

Independent work
Evaluation: give feedback to others

Ask the children to complete photocopiable page 47 'What I heard' and use it to decide how good or how much of a villain the character they questioned seemed. The children should then feed back this information to their partners.

Plenary
Display your chart about the two characters from Day 1. Consider if anything needs to be added. Highlight words in the text that the children have overlooked. For example, does *please* show how good Cinderella is? What about the Stepmother's action when the courtiers arrived? Add further ideas.

DAY 4 ■ Too good to be true?

Key features	Stages	Additional opportunities

Introduction
Display the chart from the previous day. Focus on Cinderella, the 'good' character. Suggest that the things Cinderella says and does make her seem almost too good to be true. Let the children into a secret: you have found *The True Story of Cinderella* and she is not as perfect as you all thought!
Display and read *The True Story of Cinderella* from the CD-ROM.
Highlight the dialogue and compare it with dialogue you wrote on the chart for the traditional story.

Phonics: *feet, wore*
HFW: because, ran

Support: a differentiated version of *The True Story of Cinderella* is available on the CD-ROM

Speaking and listening
Creative thinking: generate imaginative ideas

Ask the children to share ideas with a partner for some new dialogue to add to this story.

Independent work
Ask the children to write their new dialogue on their individual whiteboards.

Plenary
Social skills: listen to and respect other people's ideas

Share ideas as a class, with the children speaking their dialogue in an appropriate voice. Agree on some dialogue to add to *The True Story of Cinderella*.

DAY 5 ◼ Improving dialogue

Key features	Stages	Additional opportunities
	### Introduction Read aloud *The True Story of Cinderella* from the CD-ROM. Draw attention to its dialogue and remind the children about the previous day's work. Suggest that dialogue could still be improved. Divide the class into four groups and ask each group to focus on one of the four main characters: Cinderella, the Stepmother, the older Stepsister, the Prince.	**Phonics:** feet, wore **HFW:** because, ran
Social skills: work collaboratively	### Speaking and listening Within their groups, ask pairs of children to discuss their character's role in this story and the way she or he speaks.	
Creative thinking: generate imaginative ideas	### Independent work Ask each group of children to examine what their character says. Suggest they work with a partner and share ideas for more dialogue for their character, speaking it to each other to see if it sounds right. Ask the children to write the new dialogue in the speech bubbles on photocopiable page 48 'Cinderella characters'.	
	### Plenary Listen as children from different groups speak their words to one another. Do the other children think the words suit the characters? Put the class into pairs of different characters, so they can try out their dialogue to each other in role.	

DAY 6 ◼ Making links

Key features	Stages	Additional opportunities
	### Introduction Display *The True Story of Cinderella* from the CD-ROM and highlight the connectives. Remind the children about a connective's function: to make a link between the sentence that has gone before and the one coming next. Examine how the highlighted connectives fulfil this function. List the different connectives used in the text.	**Phonics:** hate, girl **HFW:** too, your
Social skills: work collaboratively	### Speaking and listening Ask the children to work with their partners and make up two oral sentences about events from another traditional story, such as *Little Red Riding Hood*. The second sentence must begin with a connective listed earlier. Ask the children to each write one of the sentences on their individual whiteboard. Share the results, asking partners to read aloud their sentences.	
Problem solving: consider a range of possible solutions	### Independent work Ask the children to complete photocopiable page 49 'Little Red Riding Hood'. They need to put a connective in each gap.	
	### Plenary Discuss the children's answers. Ask: *Does more than one connective make sense here?* Use the 'Little Red Riding Hood' interactive activity from the CD-ROM to agree on the best connectives to use in each instance.	

DAY 7 ▪ Creating tension

Key features	Stages	Additional opportunities
	Introduction Display *The True Story of Cinderella* from the CD-ROM. Remind the class of yesterday's work. Ask: *What is a connective? What job does it do?* With the children's help, highlight the connectives. Question the children about particular meanings. Ask: *What time information do* meanwhile *and* eventually *give the reader?*	**Phonics:** hate, girl **HFW:** too, your
Problem solving: consider a range of possible solutions	**Speaking and listening** Point out the repetition of *eventually* and *when.* Ask the children to discuss using an alternative somewhere. Point out that the connective can be a single word or a phrase. (For example: *finally; at last; once.*) Share ideas. Do the children think the text has been improved? Has the story become more exciting?	
	Independent work Provide copies of the middle section of the story (*After they had gone ... she ran*). Ask the children to choose four to six places to create more tension in the story by adding or substituting a good connective. (For example: *soon; in the end; after a while; straightaway; later.*)	**Support:** provide a list of possible connectives
	Plenary Listen to the new texts. Do the other children think there is more tension?	

Guided reading
Ask groups of children to read and discuss the two Cinderella stories with your teaching assistant. What differences can they identify between the two stories?

Assessment
Talk to the children about the main characters in the stories.
Ask: *What sort of character is Cinderella in each story? What evidence is there in the text?*
Refer back to the learning outcomes on page 33.

Further work
Extend the Assessment activity to look at the Stepmother.
Ask: *What sort of character is she in each story? What evidence is there in the text?*

DAY 1 ▪ Cinderella's stepmother

Key features	Stages	Additional opportunities
	Introduction Display and read the traditional tale *Cinderella* from the CD-ROM. Ask the children: *Who is the good central character? Who is the villain?* Concentrate on the Stepmother's attitude, not her words. Ask: *Does she treat Cinderella in the same way as her stepsisters?* Display the class chart of character characteristics (see Phase 1, Day 1). Suggest reversing the characteristics for the Stepmother.	**Phonics:** wh*i*te, f*air*y **HFW:** night, as
Creative thinking: generate imaginative ideas to make connections	**Speaking and listening** Ask the children, in pairs, to discuss how a 'good' Stepmother might behave towards Cinderella. Compare answers. Suggest that she might ask the stepsisters to do some of the jobs around the house to help Cinderella.	
	Independent work Using photocopiable page 50 'Cinderella's stepmother', ask the children to identify which story parts are shown. They should discuss with a partner what the Stepmother is doing in each picture. For each picture, ask them to draw her new action as a 'good' character.	
	Plenary Let children present their pictures, explaining how the Stepmother is now behaving as the 'good' character.	

DAY 2 ▪ Swapping roles

Key features	Stages	Additional opportunities
	Introduction Return to the traditional tale of *Cinderella* from the CD-ROM. Remind the children about their previous day's pictures. What did they do? How did they change the Stepmother? Is she still the villain?	**Phonics:** wh*i*te, f*air*y **HFW:** night, as
Communication: work collaboratively to discuss a traditional tale	**Speaking and listening** Ask the children to look at their pictures as you read story extracts with her dialogue. Encourage them to discuss her dialogue with a partner. Do the pictures and her words make sense together? As a class, agree that the Stepmother needs new words. Discuss what she might say. Model how to write words for a speech bubble.	
	Independent work Ask the children to choose new words for the Stepmother for their four pictures. Remind them that the Stepmother now needs to speak as the 'good' character.	**Support:** provide alternative words for the Stepmother and ask the children to choose which are most appropriate
	Plenary Listen together as the children read their words. Write some of them in speech bubbles on the board.	

DAY 3 ■ Strike a pose!

Key features	Stages	Additional opportunities
	### Introduction Adopt a pose with obvious body language – for example: a cheerful smile or hands on hips for anger. Ask the children: *What sort of mood am I in? How can you tell?* Display picture 2 from photocopiable page 50 'Cinderella's stepmother', which shows the stepsisters preparing for the ball.	**Phonics:** g*oo*d, p*o*se **HFW:** good
Communication: work collaboratively to discuss and plan a traditional tale	### Speaking and listening Ask the children to discuss the Stepmother's body language with their partners. Ask: *What is her mood?* Share ideas as a class. Ask the children to justify their opinions. Remind them that the Stepmother has become 'good'. Ask them to discuss with their partner and then model her changed look. Repeat the exercise for Cinderella, who has now become a villain. Display all four pictures from the photocopiable sheet. Point out that the main characters' body language does not suit their new roles.	
	### Independent work Ask the children to work with a partner and decide on new body language for the Stepmother and/or Cinderella, now that they have swapped roles. Encourage them to pose for each other as they prepare their presentations.	
	### Plenary Ask the children to adopt their poses as you display the pictures. Have the children changed the Stepmother to the 'good' character?	

DAY 4 ■ Expressions and gestures

Key features	Stages	Additional opportunities
	### Introduction Revise the work from yesterday. Display the pictures from photocopiable page 50 'Cinderella's stepmother'.	**Phonics:** g*oo*d, p*o*se **HFW:** good
	### Speaking and listening Ask the children to remind themselves of the body language for the Stepmother and Cinderella, and to demonstrate poses. As you highlight a key episode of the story, ask the children to demonstrate the body language that the Stepmother and/or Cinderella would be adopting.	
Creative thinking: generate imaginative ideas	### Independent work Ask the children, working in pairs, to draw their versions of the key episodes in the boxes on photocopiable page 26 'Storyboard'. Emphasise the need to change the characters' body language, making Cinderella the villain and the Stepmother the 'good' character. Their facial expressions and body language must show their new characteristics.	
Evaluation: give feedback to others	### Plenary Scan the children's work to allow them to present their pictures on screen. Encourage the other children to comment constructively on the gestures, posture and facial expressions they notice.	

DAY 5 ▪ A class story

Key features	Stages	Additional opportunities
	Introduction Before the lesson, make your own storyboard using photocopiable page 26 'Storyboard' showing body language that suits Cinderella and the Stepmother's reversed characteristics. Tell the children that you, like them, have re-drawn the key episodes of the story. Display your storyboard and read aloud some of the text from the traditional *Cinderella* story from the CD-ROM. Ask: *Are the words appropriate?* Agree that the story needs rewriting.	**Phonics:** *more, wear* **HFW:** once, lived
Communication: work collaboratively to discuss, plan and write a traditional tale	**Speaking and listening** Ask the children to discuss with a partner what to write beneath the first picture. Share ideas as a class. Write down the lines you decide on together for the first box. **Independent work** Ask the children to think of ideas for what to write beneath your other three boxes. Remind them that Cinderella is now the villain and the Stepmother is the 'good' character. **Plenary** Share the children's suggestions. Demonstrate how to write appropriate text for each episode. (Avoid the most appropriate connectives.) Finish by reading your new story aloud while looking at the pictures. Save your finished version.	

DAY 6 ▪ Matching words to pictures

Key features	Stages	Additional opportunities
	Introduction Remind the children about yesterday's work. Talk about how you decided on your text. What did you make sure of? (That the text matched the pictures.) Return the children's storyboards to them.	**Phonics:** *more, wear* **HFW:** once, lived
Communication: recognise communication in different modes	**Speaking and listening** Ask the children to discuss with a partner what they should write to suit their episode pictures. Ask them to think about whether the words will suit Cinderella and the Stepmother's new roles. **Independent work** Ask the children, in pairs or individually, to write rough drafts of their story texts, using a computer or another piece of paper. Suggest they check that the words and the pictures match.	**Support:** put the children in mixed-ability pairs so they can support each other to use the computer
Evaluation: give feedback to others	**Plenary** Let the children share their drafts by reading their texts aloud to their partners or to small groups. Encourage them to give constructive comments as the children tell one another if there are words that conflict with the pictures.	

DAY 7 ■ Making improvements

Key features	Stages	Additional opportunities
	Introduction Repeat the final Plenary task from yesterday, with children and their partners advising each other about possible text improvements. Give the children time to alter their texts, reminding them that they are only at draft stage. Revise connectives (see Phase 1, Days 6 and 7). Display your storyboard and text from Phase 1, Day 5. Read the text aloud, highlighting the connectives as the children identify them.	**Phonics:** name, wear **HFW:** when, then
Problem solving: consider a range of possible solutions	**Speaking and listening** Ask the children to talk to a partner and identify two places where they could improve their stories with a better connective. Share suggestions as a class. Demonstrate how to replace connectives.	
	Independent work Ask the children, in pairs or individually, to improve their texts by adding or replacing connectives. Stress the value of making good choices to create tension.	**Support:** work with children to identify and replace connectives
	Plenary Let the children share their final drafts with partners or small groups. Encourage them to make constructive comments as they tell one another if they know a better choice of connective.	**Extend:** challenge the children to use unusual connectives

DAY 8 ■ A new traditional tale

Key features	Stages	Additional opportunities
	Introduction Explain that the children now have their drafts. To create a final story, they must write a neat version. This could be done on another piece of paper or using the computer. The storyboard pictures could be placed alongside the text.	**Phonics:** name, wear **HFW:** when, then
	Independent work Ask the children to write their final version of their text. Remind them of the importance of good presentation.	
Creative thinking: experiment with different modes of communication	**Plenary** Organise story-reading clubs in which everyone has the chance for others to enjoy their work. Begin with pairs, then put the pairs together into fours. Finish with a class discussion. Point out that the children's stories are still traditional: the original characters have just reversed their characteristics. Which way round do the children prefer? Do they prefer the new characters or the original traditional ones? Consider letting another class enjoy seeing and reading the children's traditional stories with a difference.	

Guided writing

Demonstrate to the children how they can use the computer to present their work. Emphasise the importance of using paragraphs and starting each new section of speech on a new line.

Assessment

Assess the children's recognition that text must match character action by using the class storyboard story.
Pose questions about the villain and the central 'good' character:
Which one is which?
How can you tell?
What else would Cinderella do as a villain?
Refer back to the learning outcomes on page 33.

Further work

Extend the assessment task to focus on the Stepmother:
What suggests she is the good character?
What else would she do as a good character?
Which other character could change?

DAY 1 ■ A multimodal story

Key features	Stages	Additional opportunities
Communication: recognise communication in different modes	**Introduction** Display and read the *Cinderella* multimodal story from the CD-ROM. Encourage the children to think about the pictures. Ask: *Do they add to the words? Do they bring the words to life? How?*	**Phonics:** girl, her **HFW:** once, called
Communication: work collaboratively to discuss a traditional tale	**Speaking and listening** Concentrate on the early pages of the story. Ask the children to exchange views with their partners on which picture they think adds most to the humour of the narrative. Ask them to justify their choices. As a class, discuss the characters of Cinderella and her Stepmother. Model how to find evidence about a character from a word, image (a facial expression), or sound (the way the character speaks).	
	Independent work Run the presentation slowly. As you do this, ask the children to make notes on which word, image or sound tells them something about Cinderella or her Stepmother's character. Ask the children to decide which images or sounds add information that is not given by the words of the story.	**Support:** children can work with a partner
	Plenary Share the children's findings. Record the ideas in a character comparison chart.	

DAY 2 ■ Character comparisons

Key features	Stages	Additional opportunities
Communication: recognise communication in different modes	**Introduction** Display and read *The True Story of Cinderella* from the CD-ROM. Ask the children to think about yesterday's presentation story.	**Phonics:** hate, girl **HFW:** too, your
Communication: work collaboratively to discuss a traditional tale	**Speaking and listening** Ask the children to discuss the differences between the two stories. What is the main difference? Which do they prefer? Collect opinions as a class. Agree that *The True Story of Cinderella* relies on words. Are there more words here? Why are they needed? Ask the children to tell you how they can tell that the Stepmother speaks politely to Cinderella. (She says *please*.)	
Problem solving: consider a range of possible solutions	**Independent work** Give the children copies of *The True Story of Cinderella*. Ask them to find evidence that shows what the characters are like and to underline the evidence using separate colours for the two characters. Remind them that what characters do and say are important. If there is time, let partners transfer their results to their own character comparison chart – completing one half for Cinderella and the other half for the Stepmother.	
	Plenary Share ideas as a class, before making additions to your class character comparison chart.	

DAY 3 ■ Mental pictures

Key features	Stages	Additional opportunities
	Introduction Tell the children that you have been asked to visit a Reception class to read the children a short story, so you have written *Cinderella*. As your class listen to it, you want them to pretend to be Reception children, forming pictures of the characters in their minds.	**Phonics:** g*ir*l, h*er* **HFW:** once, called
Communication: work together to discuss and plan a traditional story	**Speaking and listening** Read aloud the text from the multimodal story of *Cinderella* from the CD-ROM, but do not display the pictures or use sound. Make your voice sympathetic to Cinderella as the 'good' character, with the Stepmother as the villain. Afterwards, discuss the class's mental pictures. If necessary, 'steer' the discussion so that the children conclude Reception will imagine a good Cinderella and a Stepmother who is a villain.	
	Independent work Now display the page pictures from the multimodal story of *Cinderella*. Let the children work with a partner to identify and note the numbers of the pages that they think are wrong for your planned traditional story: one partner could record page numbers for contradictory images, one for sounds.	
	Plenary Discuss the results. Encourage the children to talk about their reactions to the images and sounds. How do they contradict with how you want to read the text? Record the class findings on the comparison chart.	

DAY 4 ■ A new image

Key features	Stages	Additional opportunities
Communication: work together to discuss and plan a traditional story	**Introduction** Return to yesterday's scenario (creating a *Cinderella story* for Reception children). Explain that you have decided the children are right – you will have to change the pictures and sound or you run the risk of upsetting Reception by revealing the true story of Cinderella! Display the multimodal story of *Cinderella*. Select a screen and consider how the pictures might be changed – for example, how could the Stepmother's image be changed to that of a villain?	**Phonics:** g*ir*l, h*er* **HFW:** once, called
Creative thinking: generate imaginative ideas	**Speaking and listening** Ask the children to discuss the actions and speech of a nasty stepmother with their partners. Open the text-only version of the multimodal story of *Cinderella* from the CD-ROM. Share ideas as a class and make notes on the same screen about how the children want to change the pictures. Keep a copy.	
	Independent work Select a screen of the multimodal story. Independently or with a partner, ask the children to plan how the new Cinderella should look. Suggest the children make notes and a drawing. Display your class chart as a reminder of the characteristics of a good character.	
Evaluation: give feedback to others	**Plenary** Let the children present their ideas. Do others think this looks and sounds like a different Cinderella from the one shown in the original multimodal story?	

DAY 5 ▪ Changing pictures

Key features	Stages	Additional opportunities
Communication: work together to discuss and plan a traditional story	**Introduction** Display and read the whole of the multimodal story of *Cinderella* from the CD-ROM. Remind the children about yesterday's work and the class's new ideas. Build on this work, selecting different screens. Discuss further ways you could change the images of the Stepmother and Cinderella. For example, the Stepmother may look furious or have her hands on her hips when Cinderella wants to wear her party dress.	**Phonics:** her, were **HFW:** ball, but
Creative thinking: generate imaginative ideas	**Speaking and listening** Ask the children, in small groups, to discuss using sounds and images on these screens to present the Stepmother and Cinderella differently. Share ideas as a class. Agree changes, and add notes about new images on the screens.	
	Independent work As you display other screens of the story, ask the children, in small groups, to decide on sounds and changes to images to be added or made. Ask the children to record their ideas in notes and sketches.	
	Plenary Share some of the ideas. Make other suggestions that the children have not thought of.	

DAY 6 ▪ Freeze-frame photos

Key features	Stages	Additional opportunities
	Introduction Explain to the class that they are going to continue making their own multimodal stories.	**Phonics:** her, were **HFW:** ball, sister
Communication: work together to discuss, plan and create a traditional story	**Speaking and listening** The children should finish deciding on images. Remind them of how we gain information about characters from their body language. Consider using freeze-framing – children can act out their images and then take photographs. (Ensure to get parents' or carers' permission before taking photographs.) Bring the class together to model how to add images to the presentation text. After discussing what the characters are saying and thinking, model how to record sound text, making the voice suit the character and then adding it to the story. (For example, the stepsister could say, *No, you're too young* in a sneering voice.) Make changes to the story so that words, sounds and images work together.	
Creative thinking: experiment with different modes of communication	**Independent work** Ask the children, in their small groups, to discuss and write what each character thinks or says. Using their photographs or drawn images, the children should import images, and record the sound text and add it to their presentations.	
Evaluation: judge the effectiveness of their own work	**Plenary** Ask the children to evaluate their final stories. Are they happy with them? Give each group the chance to present their finished story to another group.	

Guided reading

Working in small groups with your teaching assistant, let the children read the plain text version of *The True Story of Cinderella.* Ask them to plan and make some freeze-frame images that could accompany parts of the text.

Assessment

Use *The True Story of Little Red Riding Hood* photocopiable assessment activity from the CD-ROM. When children have completed the activity, question them about their drawings: *What impressions do they give of the character? How are the impressions different from the text?* Refer back to the learning outcomes on page 33.

Further work

Extend the assessment task by asking the children:
What changes would you make to the images so that they matched the text? How would you make those changes? Could sounds help?

What I heard

I listened to _____

My partner was acting as _____ (Cinderella or the Stepmother)

These words sounded like the character: _____

_____

_____

_____

The words proved the character was a _____

(good person or villain)

NARRATIVE ■ UNIT 2

Cinderella characters

■ What might these characters say? Write words in the speech bubbles.

PHOTOCOPIABLE

■ SCHOLASTIC
www.scholastic.co.uk

Little Red Riding Hood

■ Fill the gaps with connectives from the box. You may want to use some of them more than once.

Once upon a time Little Red Riding Hood went into the forest. She carried a basket of food for Granny. _____ she became tired and she sat down to rest. _____ she fell fast asleep.

_____ Big Bad Wolf was searching for food. He saw the little girl. _____ she woke up he heard her say, "Off I go to Granny's!"

_____ Big Bad Wolf raced ahead to Granny's cottage. _____ he got there, he knocked at the door. _____ he heard a voice.

"Come in," called Granny.

The wolf went in and gobbled up Granny.

_____ Little Red Riding Hood was still walking along the path. _____ she arrived at Granny's cottage. _____ she was going to knock at the door, she heard a strange noise.

_____ she made up her mind to look through the window. What do you think she saw?

Connectives

when	then	meanwhile	eventually	just as	next	soon

Cinderella's stepmother

PHOTOCOPIABLE ■SCHOLASTIC
www.scholastic.co.uk

Illustration © Neil Chapman/Beehive Illustration.

NARRATIVE
UNIT 3 Different stories by the same author

Speak and listen for a range of purposes on paper and on screen

Strand 2 Listening and responding
■ Listen to others in class, ask relevant questions and follow instructions.
Strand 3 Group discussion and interaction
■ Work effectively in groups by ensuring that each group member takes a turn challenging, supporting and moving on.
Strand 4 Drama
■ Adopt appropriate roles in small or large groups and consider alternative courses of action.

Read for a range of purposes on paper and on screen

Strand 5 Word recognition: decoding (reading) and encoding (spelling)
■ Read independently and with increasing fluency longer and less familiar texts.
■ Spell with increasing accuracy and confidence, drawing on word recognition and knowledge of word structure and spelling patterns.
■ Know how to tackle unfamiliar words that are not completely decodable.
■ Read and spell less common alternative graphemes including trigraphs.
■ Read high and medium frequency words independently and automatically.
Strand 6 Word structure and spelling
■ Spell with increasing accuracy and confidence, drawing on word recognition and knowledge of word structure, and spelling patterns including common inflections and use of double letters.
■ Read and spell less common alternative graphemes including trigraphs.
Strand 8 Engaging with and responding to texts
■ Engage with books through exploring and enacting interpretations.
■ Explain their reactions to texts, commenting on important aspects.

Write for a range of purposes on paper and on screen

Strand 9 Creating and shaping texts
Sustain form in narrative, including use of person and time.
Strand 10 Text structure and organisation
Use planning to establish clear sections for writing.
Strand 11 Sentence structure and punctuation
Compose sentences using tense consistently (present and past).

Progression in narrative

In this year, children are moving towards:
■ Understanding elements of an author's style.
■ Understanding that we know what characters are like from what they say and do as well as their appearance; making predictions about how they might behave; understanding that the way that characters speak reflects their personality and that the verbs used for dialogue tell us how a character is feeling.

▶

UNIT 3 ◄ Different stories by the same author *continued*

Key aspects of learning covered in this Unit

Reasoning
Children will compare texts and give evidence for the opinions they form.
Evaluation
As they learn about features of an author's style, children will become better equipped to make judgements about the type of books they enjoy reading.
Social skills
Children participate in a collaborative group activity. They will learn about taking turns, listening to others and reaching agreement.
Communication
Children will develop their ability to discuss as they work collaboratively in paired, group and whole-class contexts. They will communicate outcomes orally, in writing and through ICT if appropriate.

Prior learning

Before starting this Unit check that the children can:
■ Identify typical features of a traditional story.
■ Demonstrate understanding of characterisation by talking about what a character looks like, how the character behaves and suggesting reasons for the character's feelings or actions.
■ Write a complete story using a shared story plan, making use of features from reading to make it 'sound like a story'.
■ Present a logical sequence of events and make use of connectives to show links between events.
If they need further support please refer to a prior Unit or a similar Unit in Year 1.

Resources

Phase 1:
A range of books by Francesca Simon, to create a display; *Horrid Henry's Sports Day* by Francesca Simon ✦; *Horrid Henry's School Trip* by Francesca Simon ✦; *Horrid Henry and the Demon Dinner Lady* by Francesca Simon ✦; Photocopiable page 65 'Book review'
Phase 2:
Horrid Henry's Sports Day by Francesca Simon ✦
Phase 3:
A range of books by Humphrey Carpenter, to create a display; *Mr Majeika and the Music Teacher* by Humphrey Carpenter ✦; Photocopiable page 66 'Book evaluation'
Phase 4:
Horrid Henry's School Trip by Francesca Simon ✦; Photocopiable page 67 'What did Henry say?'; Photocopiable page 68 'Listen to Henry's voice'; Photocopiable page 29 'Story planner'; Assessment activity 'Mrs Magic's Hat' ✦

Cross-curricular opportunities

ICT – Finding information

UNIT 3 ■ Teaching sequence

Phase	Children's objectives	Summary of activities	Learning outcomes
1	I can comment on important aspects in a text.	Review a story by Francesca Simon. Make comparisons by reviewing another story by the same author. Use book blurb and the internet to find out about the author. Identify characteristics of the author's style.	Children can talk about a text and explain their reaction to it.
2	I can use evidence in the text to talk about a character.	Investigate character by asking questions and answering them in role. Explore how a character's behaviour can change in the course of a story.	Children can make inferences about characters and use the text to support their answers.
3	I can read a whole book. I can work as part of a group.	Research a different author. Read a complete book. Hold group discussions about the books read and agree which one should receive a prize.	Children can work as a member of a group to discuss and reach agreement over a task.
4	I can use what I read to help me write.	Discuss ideas for a new story and its main characters. Write new dialogue for a character. Plan and write a complete story.	Children can plan and write a sustained story about a familiar character. Children can use the past tense and third person, and can include some dialogue and detail to add interest.

Provide copies of the objectives for the children.

DAY 1 ▨ Studying Francesca Simon

Key features	Stages	Additional opportunities
	Introduction Create a display of books by Francesca Simon. Include books and short stories by her that the children will be able to read independently during the course of this Unit. Point out the author's name on a cover. Ask the children: *Have you heard of this author? What sort of books does she write?* Provide a context for *Horrid Henry's Sports Day* by telling the children about the egg-and-spoon races you took part in when you were at school. Then display and read the extract from the CD-ROM.	**Phonics:** gr*ow*led, sp*oo*n **HFW:** how, once
Communication: develop their ability to discuss; communicate outcomes orally	**Speaking and listening** Ask the children to share their immediate reactions to the story with a partner. What was happening? Which part did they enjoy? Was it funny? Discuss the story as a class, before you re-read it, emphasising important, funny or mysterious moments.	
Evaluation: make judgements about books	**Independent work** Ask the children to pretend to be book reviewers by filling in one half of photocopiable page 65 'Book review'.	**Extend:** children can type up their book reviews to appear in your school magazine
	Plenary Ask the children to express some of their opinions. Take a poll of scores for the story. How well does the story do?	

DAY 2 ▨ Comparing two stories

Key features	Stages	Additional opportunities
	Introduction Ask the children if they can remember the name of yesterday's author. Explain that you are going to read an extract from another story by her. Without supplying the title, read aloud *Horrid Henry's School Trip* from the CD-ROM.	**Phonics:** b*or*ing, h*ow*led **HFW:** or, don't
Reasoning: compare texts and give evidence for the opinions they form	**Speaking and listening** Ask the children to discuss with a partner what they notice about this author. Who or what does she like writing about? Display the text and re-read it. As a class, discuss how it is similar to yesterday's story (characters and setting) and how it differs from it (new plot).	**Support:** suggest *true* and *false* statements for the children to choose between
Evaluation: make judgements about books	**Independent work** Ask the children to fill in the second half of photocopiable page 65 'Book review'. They must think about, decide and write down which story they preferred and why.	
	Plenary Ask the children to vote for the story they preferred. Encourage the children to justify their choices.	

DAY 3 ■ Finding out more

Key features	Stages	Additional opportunities
	### Introduction Begin by asking the children: *What do you know about Francesca Simon? How can we find out more?* Point out the author's biography, which is usually on the book's inside cover. Read the biography from one of your display books.	**Phonics:** note, *out* **HFW:** live, called
Social skills: participate in a collaborative group activity	### Speaking and listening Encourage the children to discuss with their partner how they could find out more about this author. Share ideas. Suggest using the internet for information. Demonstrate this by typing in the author's name and displaying the list of results. Open some of these websites. Set some tasks for the children to complete together. For example: finding her date of birth, where she lived as a child, where she lives now, whether or not she has any pets. Make class notes on interesting information the children find out and add these notes to your Francesca Simon display.	
	### Independent work Direct the children to suitable websites: for example www.francescasimon.com and www.storiesfromtheweb.org (the '7–11' site includes an interview with Francesca Simon). Ask the children: *What interesting information can you find about this author?*	**Support:** children can work with an adult to search for information
	### Plenary Ask the children to relate their most interesting information and make notes on the board. Agree on the information that you will add to your display.	

DAY 4 ■ A new story

Key features	Stages	Additional opportunities
	### Introduction Tell the children that you are going to read them an extract from a different book today. Do not reveal the author's name. Read aloud *Horrid Henry and the Demon Dinner Lady* from the CD-ROM but keep secret the title and the author's name.	**Phonics:** m*ar*ched, f*oo*d **HFW:** away, there
	### Speaking and listening Ask the children in pairs or small groups to discuss what they have just heard. Do they recognise the book? Do they recognise the writer? How? Share ideas as a class. Reveal the author's name. Display the text and re-read it.	
Evaluation: learn about features of an author's style	### Independent work Ask the children, in pairs or small groups, to discuss how they can recognise this author's style. Suggest they make notes and write down words in the text that are distinctive of this author's books.	**Support:** print copies of the text for children to underline the words they identify
Communication: develop their ability to discuss	### Plenary Ask one child from each pair or group to explain their findings. Collaborate to create a chart listing important aspects of Francesca Simon's style.	

Guided reading

Give the children a short story by Francesca Simon to read in a group. Help them to think about the story by asking: *How was it similar to her other stories? Did it differ from her other stories?*

Assessment

Assess the children's recognition of the author's style by asking: *What do you enjoy about this author's books? How is she special? Which story or section have you enjoyed?* Refer back to the learning outcomes on page 53.

Further work

Suggest that the children compare Francesca Simon's books to an author they usually read. Ask: *How do the styles differ? Do they prefer one author? Why?*

DAY 1 ■ About a boy

Key features	Stages	Additional opportunities
	Introduction Remind the children about the *Horrid Henry* stories. Read aloud *Horrid Henry's Sports Day* from the CD-ROM.	**Phonics:** gr*ow*led, sn*ar*led **HFW:** how, once
Communication: work collaboratively in whole-class contexts	**Speaking and listening** Ask the children to think about the sort of person Henry is, before telling a partner something they have learned about him from the extract. Share ideas as a class. Draw an outline of a boy, to represent Henry, on the board. Use some of the ideas to write notes on what you already know about this character, writing the notes inside the Henry outline. Keep a copy for tomorrow's session.	
	Independent work Ask the children to imagine that Henry is going to visit the classroom tomorrow and they children will be able to question him. Encourage them to think of and write down three questions that will help them learn more about Henry.	**Support:** children can work with an adult to think of one question to ask
Social skills: listening to others and reaching agreement	**Plenary** Listen to the children's questions. Explain that you only want to use the ones that are likely to provide interesting answers. Encourage constructive criticism as the children help in the selection. Write the chosen questions the around your drawing of Henry. Keep a copy.	

DAY 2 ■ Henry in the hot-seat

Key features	Stages	Additional opportunities
	Introduction Display and read together *Horrid Henry's Sports Day* from the CD-ROM, explaining that you want to look for clues about Henry's thoughts and feelings. Highlight *growled* and *snarled,* verbs used to link Henry's dialogue. Ask *What do the verbs tell us about Henry's feelings?*	**Phonics:** gr*ow*led, sn*ar*led **HFW:** how, once
Communication: work collaboratively in whole-class contexts	**Speaking and listening** Ask partners to share ideas on other words (often verbs) in the extract that are clues about Henry's feelings. Discuss ideas as a class. Highlight words the children mention. Ask: *What do these words tell the reader about Henry's thoughts? How was he feeling?* Remind the children about Henry's impending visit! Return to your drawing of Henry and re-read the questions you wanted to ask him.	
	Independent work Give the children some cut-out speech bubbles. Ask the children to take the part of Henry themselves and to think how he would answer the questions. They can write the answers they think he would give in the speech bubbles.	**Support:** ask the children to choose between two alternative answers
Social skills: taking turns and listening to others	**Plenary** Ask children to take it in turns to hot-seat Henry, reading their answers to the questions.	

DAY 3 ◼ Meet the family

Key features	Stages	Additional opportunities
	### Introduction Display *Horrid Henry's Sports Day* from the CD-ROM and read it together. Talk with the children about the other characters in the story. Ask: *Who else in this part of the story? Does the author make them seem as important as Henry?*	**Phonics:** growled, snarled **HFW:** how, once
Communication: work collaboratively in paired contexts	### Speaking and listening Ask the children to discuss with their partners how Perfect Peter feels in this episode. Can they identify a word that gives a clue to his feelings? Share ideas as a class.	
	### Independent work Put the children into groups of three. Explain that each member of the group must take the part of a family member: Henry, Peter or Mum. You want them to act out the scene. They can improvise their own dialogue. Every so often while the children are acting, call out *Freeze!* Each group must freeze in position, as you try to tell which part of the scene is shown and what characters are feeling.	
Social skills: taking turns and listening to others	### Plenary Let one group act the scene as the rest of you watch. Freeze the action at a critical point, and ask the characters to explain what their character is thinking or feeling at that point. Ask members of the audience to stand next to one of the characters and speak what is in the character's mind.	

DAY 4 ◼ Changing characters

Key features	Stages	Additional opportunities
	### Introduction Remind the children that you have been finding out about characters. Ask them: *Does a character have to stay the same throughout a story?* Remind the children of stories where the main character's personality or behaviour has changed. Display and read together *Horrid Henry's Sports Day* from the CD-ROM.	**Phonics:** growled, snarled **HFW:** how, once
Communication: work collaboratively in paired contexts	### Speaking and listening Use partner discussion to focus on the characters of Peter and Mum. What sort of people do they seem to be?	
	### Independent work If possible obtain the book and read the children the end of the Sports Day story. (Peter gets in trouble with the teacher; Mum is shouted at by a parent.) Ask the children to write about: ■ Peter's feelings in the early part of the story (the text extract) ■ his probable feelings at the end and how they have changed ■ how Peter will behave in the future.	**Extend:** children can write their notes in the form of an entry in Peter's diary
Communication: communicate outcomes orally	### Plenary Discuss Henry and what happens to him at the end of the story. (He wins the trophy.) Would the children have predicted that? Will his behaviour change in future? (Compare this story with *The True Story of Cinderella* from Unit 1, where the character of Cinderella learns and changes.)	

Guided writing

Work with groups of children to create a timeline of how Henry's behaviour changes throughout the story and include the events that cause these changes to take place.

Assessment

Assess the children understanding of Henry's character, by asking:

What sort of person is Henry?
Why do you think that?
What evidence is there in the story?
Refer back to the learning outcomes on page 53.

Further work

Encourage the children to investigate Henry's character more closely in this story. Ask:

Can you identify any changes in him during the story?
Do the other characters change?

DAY 1 ■ Studying Humphrey Carpenter

Key features	Stages	Additional opportunities
	### Introduction Ask the children if they remember good ways to find out about an author. Remind them of the research sources you used in Phase 1: ■ book blurb and author biography; ■ websites. Suggest that their own and other people's experiences of reading an author's books can also be a useful source of information.	**Phonics:** book **HFW:** by
	### Speaking and listening Ask the children to tell each other how they found information about Francesca Simon and her books.	
Communication: work collaboratively in group contexts	### Independent work Create a display of books by Humphrey Carpenter. Working in small groups, encourage the children to find out about Humphrey Carpenter using the books and the internet. Suggest they look at websites such as the 'Authors' section of www.penguin.co.uk (be aware that a lot of the sites that appear in a general search will contain obituaries). Encourage the children to make notes and decide how they will present their findings to the rest of the class.	**Support:** prepare a sheet of questions about Humphrey Carpenter for children to answer
Communication: communicate outcomes orally	### Plenary Ask the groups to make their reports. Can you add any information that every group has missed?	

DAY 2 ■ A good read

Key features	Stages	Additional opportunities
	### Introduction Remind the children about the new author you are studying.	**Phonics:** book **HFW:** by
	### Speaking and listening Ask the children to remind a partner of what they know about Humphrey Carpenter.	
Evaluation: make judgements about books	### Independent work Give the children the exciting news that they are going to have the chance to each read a complete book by Humphrey Carpenter! Allow time for the children, using partner reading if necessary, to read one complete book. Make sure that each child 'reads' a complete book, but adapt the task if necessary: ■ an adult could read aloud/paraphrase sections of the book; ■ individual children could read one or two chapters, and then confer to piece together the complete book. Make sure that more than one of Carpenter's books is being studied within the class. Ask the children to complete photocopiable page 66 'Book evaluation'.	
	### Plenary Ask the children about their progress. Did they find it easy to sustain interest in a complete book?	

DAY 3 ■ And the winner is...

Key features	Stages	Additional opportunities

Introduction
Remind the children of their book evaluations.

Speaking and listening
Put the children into groups or pairs where each child has evaluated a different book.

Reasoning: compare texts and give evidence for the opinions they form

Ask the children to hold group discussions, telling one another about their books. Can they identify any common features? (Perhaps something funny always happened.)

They must decide which book to recommend to the class.

Come together as a class and ask each group to report their recommendations. Is there a clear winner of the Year 2 Bookworm Prize?

Communication: communicate outcomes orally

Working again in their earlier groups or pairs, ask the children to reflect on how their talk helped them to reach agreement on which book to recommend to the class. They may need adult support.

Plenary
Share ideas as a class, making a chart of some of the benefits of discussion when a group has to reach agreement.

Additional opportunities

Phonics: b*oo*k, pr*i*ze
HFW: by, who, or

Guided reading
Display *Mr Majeika and the Music Teacher* from the CD-ROM and read it together as a class.
Suggest that the children share opinions in a group. Do they think this may be an important early part of the story. Why?

Assessment
Return to the guided reading groups. Let the groups discuss whether to recommend this (or a different Humphrey Carpenter book) to the class. Assess the children's ability to:
■ make a valid contribution in a discussion in a collaborative group activity;
■ recognise the need to listen to others and reach agreement,
Refer back to the learning outcomes on page 53.

Further work
Let the children progress to reading a second complete story by Humphrey Carpenter.
Again, they can discuss and reach agreement with others about whether or not they would recommend it to the rest of the class.

DAY 1 ■ A new character

Key features	Stages	Additional opportunities
	Introduction Remind the children about the character, Horrid Henry. Ask them: *What sort of person is he? What sort of things does he do?* Remind the children of book titles they know in the Horrid Henry series.	**Phonics:** Nora **HFW:** take, sister
Communication: work collaboratively in a whole-class context	**Speaking and listening** Ask the children to talk to a partner about a new title for a book about a new fictional character, Naughty Nora. Share ideas as a class. Write a title for a class story on the board, for example, *Naughty Nora Visits the Doctor*. Make a class list of ideas for how Nora will behave in the doctor's surgery. (For example: she could refuse to take her jumper off; put fake spots on herself; write her own prescription; manage to make her sister, Angelic Alice, have two hearing tests, but herself none.)	
Social skills: learn about listening to others	**Independent work** Put the children into small groups. Ask them to discuss ideas for this story, using improvisation and role play to try them out. Encourage them to explore alternative courses of action.	
	Plenary Ask group representatives to explain their ideas. Make a note of them and save them for children to refer to later.	

DAY 2 ■ Henry's dialogue

Key features	Stages	Additional opportunities
	Introduction Remind the children that they have been thinking about Horrid Henry. Ask them: *What does his voice sound like?*	**Phonics:** school, howled **HFW:** or, don't
Communication: work collaboratively in paired and whole-class contexts	**Speaking and listening** Ask the children to speak to their partners as Henry. For example: he could be answering the register, or trying to persuade the teacher to put him in the football team. Point out the need to consider what he says as well as how his voice sounds. Encourage the children to make notes in the first two columns of photocopiable page 68 'Listen to Henry's voice!'. Share ideas as a class, before examining Henry's dialogue in the extract from *Horrid Henry's School Trip* from the CD-ROM. Highlight *said* and *howled*. Suggest that *howled* tells them how he spoke, but *said* lets them imagine. Ask the children: *What do you imagine? Why?* Highlight other dialogue link verbs. Question the children about these verbs. Make sure that they recognise that these verbs are in the past tense because the story is set in the past. Children can now complete the third column of photocopiable page 68 'Listen to Henry's voice!'.	
Communication: communicate outcomes orally and in writing	**Independent work** Ask the children, with their partners, to continue Henry's dialogue when he arrived at school. Suggest they try out ideas orally before writing Henry's dialogue on photocopiable page 67 'What did Henry say?'.	**Support:** ask your teaching assistant to prompt children with suggestions of what could happen
	Plenary Ask children to speak their dialogue. Do the listeners recognise Henry?	

DAY 3 ■ Discussing and planning

Key features	Stages	Additional opportunities
	Introduction Tell the children that they are now going to start work on a story featuring the new character, Naughty Nora. Refer back to the ideas that the children developed in drama on Day 1 and display the notes that you made and saved.	**Phonics:** Nora **HFW:** next, now
Communication: work collaboratively in paired and whole-class contexts	**Speaking and listening** Put the children back into the groups from Day 1 and allow time for them to discuss their ideas. Bring them back together as a class and model how to plan a story. Write four headings on the board: ■ Opening ■ Something happens ■ Events to sort it out ■ Ending Demonstrate how to make planning notes. Talk about the need to make links between each event and remind the children of the lists of connectives they have used in other stories (Unit 2, Phase 1 and photocopiable page 49).	**Support:** children can draw pictures to support their planning
	Independent work Ask the children to plan their Naughty Nora stories on photocopiable page 29 'Story planner'.	**Extend:** ask the children to put a contrasting character into their stories (such as Angelic Alice)
	Plenary Let the children read their plan to a partner. Encourage them to help each other with constructive advice.	

DAY 4 ■ Naughty Nora stories

Key features	Stages	Additional opportunities
	Introduction Remind the children of their plans. Display one of the Francesca Simon story extracts from the CD-ROM. Draw attention to the author's use of dialogue, the third person and the past tense.	**Phonics:** Nora **HFW:** next, now, said
	Independent work Ask the children to use their plans to write a sustained story about Naughty Nora. Encourage them to include dialogue and to choose words carefully when describing people and places. Remind them to keep re-reading and checking they have used the third person and the past tense consistently.	
	Speaking and listening Ask the children to read their finished story to a partner and then make changes and improvements.	
Communication: communicate outcomes in writing and through ICT	**Independent work** Provide word-processing facilities so that the children can publish their stories.	**Extend:** children can create a cover for their stories and write a blurb
	Plenary Listen as children tell the class their stories about the new character.	

Guided reading

Provide the opportunity for the children to read a Francesca Simon story in a group with your teaching assistant. Ask them to identify the story's main events. How does the author link events? Challenge the children to identify the connectives she uses.

Assessment

Use the *Mrs. Magic's Hat* interactive assessment activity from the CD-ROM. Assess if the children can put pictures and their accompanying text in the right order to tell a story.
Refer back to the learning outcomes on page 53.

Further work

Suggest that the children plan and write a new, complete story about a familiar fictional character. Remind them to include descriptions of the character and setting and some dialogue.

Book review

Book title: ⎯⎯⎯⎯⎯⎯⎯⎯⎯⎯⎯⎯⎯⎯⎯⎯⎯⎯⎯⎯⎯⎯⎯⎯⎯

Author: ⎯⎯⎯⎯⎯⎯⎯⎯⎯⎯⎯⎯⎯⎯⎯⎯⎯⎯⎯⎯⎯⎯⎯⎯⎯⎯⎯

The main character: ⎯⎯⎯⎯⎯⎯⎯⎯⎯⎯⎯⎯⎯⎯⎯⎯⎯⎯⎯⎯⎯

What happened to this character: ⎯⎯⎯⎯⎯⎯⎯⎯⎯⎯⎯⎯⎯⎯

⎯⎯⎯⎯⎯⎯⎯⎯⎯⎯⎯⎯⎯⎯⎯⎯⎯⎯⎯⎯⎯⎯⎯⎯⎯⎯⎯⎯⎯⎯⎯⎯⎯⎯⎯

⎯⎯⎯⎯⎯⎯⎯⎯⎯⎯⎯⎯⎯⎯⎯⎯⎯⎯⎯⎯⎯⎯⎯⎯⎯⎯⎯⎯⎯⎯⎯⎯⎯⎯⎯

⎯⎯⎯⎯⎯⎯⎯⎯⎯⎯⎯⎯⎯⎯⎯⎯⎯⎯⎯⎯⎯⎯⎯⎯⎯⎯⎯⎯⎯⎯⎯⎯⎯⎯⎯

⎯⎯⎯⎯⎯⎯⎯⎯⎯⎯⎯⎯⎯⎯⎯⎯⎯⎯⎯⎯⎯⎯⎯⎯⎯⎯⎯⎯⎯⎯⎯⎯⎯⎯⎯

A good word to describe this story: ⎯⎯⎯⎯⎯⎯⎯⎯⎯⎯⎯⎯⎯

Out of 10, I give it a score of ⎯⎯⎯⎯⎯⎯⎯⎯⎯⎯⎯⎯⎯⎯⎯⎯

Book title: ⎯⎯⎯⎯⎯⎯⎯⎯⎯⎯⎯⎯⎯⎯⎯⎯⎯⎯⎯⎯⎯⎯⎯⎯⎯

Author: ⎯⎯⎯⎯⎯⎯⎯⎯⎯⎯⎯⎯⎯⎯⎯⎯⎯⎯⎯⎯⎯⎯⎯⎯⎯⎯⎯

The main character: ⎯⎯⎯⎯⎯⎯⎯⎯⎯⎯⎯⎯⎯⎯⎯⎯⎯⎯⎯⎯⎯

What happened to this character: ⎯⎯⎯⎯⎯⎯⎯⎯⎯⎯⎯⎯⎯⎯

⎯⎯⎯⎯⎯⎯⎯⎯⎯⎯⎯⎯⎯⎯⎯⎯⎯⎯⎯⎯⎯⎯⎯⎯⎯⎯⎯⎯⎯⎯⎯⎯⎯⎯⎯

⎯⎯⎯⎯⎯⎯⎯⎯⎯⎯⎯⎯⎯⎯⎯⎯⎯⎯⎯⎯⎯⎯⎯⎯⎯⎯⎯⎯⎯⎯⎯⎯⎯⎯⎯

⎯⎯⎯⎯⎯⎯⎯⎯⎯⎯⎯⎯⎯⎯⎯⎯⎯⎯⎯⎯⎯⎯⎯⎯⎯⎯⎯⎯⎯⎯⎯⎯⎯⎯⎯

⎯⎯⎯⎯⎯⎯⎯⎯⎯⎯⎯⎯⎯⎯⎯⎯⎯⎯⎯⎯⎯⎯⎯⎯⎯⎯⎯⎯⎯⎯⎯⎯⎯⎯⎯

A good word to describe this story: ⎯⎯⎯⎯⎯⎯⎯⎯⎯⎯⎯⎯⎯

Out of 10, I give it a score of ⎯⎯⎯⎯⎯⎯⎯⎯⎯⎯⎯⎯⎯⎯⎯⎯

Book evaluation

Book title: _____

Author: _____

The character I liked best: _____

_____

What went wrong: _____

_____

How the problem was sorted out: _____

_____

The funniest part: _____

_____

The sort of reader who would enjoy this book: _____

_____

This book deserves a _____ award (gold, silver
or bronze).

 ■ 100 LITERACY FRAMEWORK LESSONS YEAR 2

What did Henry say?

" _____

_____ ," shouted Henry.

" _____

_____ ," he screamed.

" _____

_____ ," he said

" _____

_____ ,"

Henry _____

Listen to Henry's voice!

■ Choose some examples of Henry talking. Complete the first two columns in the table to show what he was talking about and how he sounded (for example, *angry* or *jealous*). In the third column, write a verb that you might use to describe the way Henry talked (for example, *shouted* or *shrieked*).

What was he talking about?	How did he sound?	What verb can replace said?
1. He wanted the teacher to pick him for the school football team.	He was	
2.		
3.		
4.		

NARRATIVE
UNIT 4 Extended stories/Significant authors

Speak and listen for a range of purposes on paper and on screen

Strand 2 Listening and responding
- Respond to presentations by describing characters, repeating some highlights and commenting constructively.

Strand 4 Drama
- Present part of traditional stories, their own stories or work drawn from different parts of the curriculum for members of their own class.

Read for a range of purposes on paper and on screen

Strand 5 Word recognition: decoding (reading) and encoding (spelling)
- Read independently and with increasing fluency longer and less familiar texts.
- Spell with increasing accuracy and confidence, drawing on word recognition and knowledge of word structure, and spelling patterns.
- Know how to tackle unfamiliar words that are not completely decodable.
- Read and spell less common alternative graphemes including trigraphs.
- Read high and medium frequency words independently and automatically.

Strand 6 Word structure and spelling
- Spell with increasing accuracy and confidence, drawing on word recognition and knowledge of word structure, and spelling patterns including between inflections and use of double letters.
- Read and spell less common alternative graphemes including trigraphs.

Strand 7 Understanding and interpreting texts
- Give some reasons why things happen or characters change.

Strand 8 Engaging with and responding to texts
- Engage with books through exploring and enacting interpretations.

Write for a range of purposes on paper and on screen

Strand 9 Creating and shaping texts
- Sustain form in narrative, including use of person and time.
- Select from different presentational features to suit particular writing purposes on paper and on screen.

Strand 10 Text structure and organisation
- Use appropriate language to make sections hang together.

Strand 11 Sentence structure and punctuation
- Compose sentences using tense consistently (present and past).

Strand 12 Presentation
- Word-process short narrative and non-narrative texts.

Progression in narrative

In this year, children are moving towards:
- Identifying the sequence: opening – something happens – events to sort it out – ending; identifying temporal connectives and talking about how they are used to signal the passing of time; making deductions about why events take place in a particular order by looking at characters' actions and their consequences.
- Understanding that we know what characters are like from what they say and do as well as their appearance; predicting how they might behave;

understanding that the way that characters speak reflects their personality and that the verbs used for dialogue tell us how a character is feeling.

■ Exploring characters' feelings and situations using improvisation; dramatising parts of familiar stories and performing to class or groups.

Key aspects of learning covered in this Unit

Evaluation
Children will discuss success criteria for their written work, give feedback to others and judge the quality of their own writing.

Social skills
When developing collaborative writing children will learn about listening to and respecting other people's ideas.

Self-awareness
As they work on an extended piece of writing children will learn how to organise their own work and how to maintain their concentration to complete a polished story.

Communication
Children will develop their ability to discuss as they work collaboratively in paired, group and whole-class contexts. They will communicate outcomes orally, in writing and through ICT if appropriate.

Prior learning

Before starting this Unit check that the children can:
■ Explain reasons for events in stories with reference to characters' actions and motives.
■ Work collaboratively in a group, taking turns and reaching agreement.
■ Identify story elements: characters, setting, and key events.
■ Plan a story by making notes under the headings – opening, something happens, events to sort it out, ending.
■ Write simple and compound sentences.
■ Use temporal connectives.
■ Use the third person and past tense consistently in narrative writing.
If they need further support please refer to a prior Unit or a similar Unit in Year 1.

Resources

Phase 1:
Stanley and the Magic Lamp (Part 1) by Jeff Brown ✇; *Stanley and the Magic Lamp (Part 2)* by Jeff Brown ✇; Photocopiable page 86 'All about Stanley'
Phase 2:
Stanley and the Magic Lamp (Part 1) by Jeff Brown ✇; Photocopiable page 87 'Mix and match storyboard'; Photocopiable page 29 'Story planner'
Phase 3:
Photocopiable page 88 'Theatre critic'; Assessment activity 'Label the story' ✇

Cross-curricular opportunities

ICT – Writing stories; Creating pictures

UNIT 4 ■ Teaching sequence

Phase	Children's objectives	Summary of activities	Learning outcomes
1	I can make predictions about a story. I can discuss the way characters develop.	Note the contents the opening and second episode of a story. Identify key events and how they are linked. Role play and improvise dialogue. Predict what will happen. Use speech bubbles to convey a character's thoughts and feelings. Mark an extended story against a checklist. Evaluate an extended story.	Children can make predictions about a text and discuss the way characters develop across a story.
2	I can plan and write a complete story.	Use a picture storyboard to plan a story. Write a story plan. Make a checklist for an extended story. Write a story opening. Write own extended story. Add temporal connectives to the story. Use a checklist to improve the story. Present finished story.	Children can plan a story that has a logical sequence of events. Children can write an extended narrative with: ■ a logical sequence of events ■ sentences grouped together ■ temporal connectives ■ consistent use of the third person and past tense.
3	I can work with a group to plan and present a dramatisation. I can comment on other dramatisations.	Plan, rehearse and present a group dramatisation. Respond to other group dramatisations.	Children can work as a member of a group to present a scene from a known story to an audience. Children can respond to presentations by making constructive comments.

Note: Phases 1 and 2 are designed to run concurrently so that children hear an extended text read aloud while also having the opportunity to write a longer story themselves.

Provide copies of the objectives for the children.

DAY 1 ■ Phase 1: Introducing the story

Key features	Stages	Additional opportunities
	Introduction Introduce an extended story, such as *Stanley and the Magic Lamp,* as a serial. Explain that the children will look in detail at four main parts of the story. Ask them to identify the four parts of any story – opening; something happens; events to sort out; ending. Read aloud *Stanley and the Magic Lamp (Part 1)* from the CD-ROM. This is the opening of the story.	**Phonics:** wore, year **HFW:** brother, home
Communication: work collaboratively in paired contexts	**Speaking and listening** Encourage the children to discuss with their partners whether or not they think this is a successful opening and to explain their opinions. Does the author make them want to read on? Display and re-read the text.	
	Independent work Ask the children to make notes about what the author tells the reader in this opening. They should check if the author answers the important *wh-* questions: *Who? Where? What? Why? When?*	**Support:** children can work in pairs **Extend:** children can suggest what else the author should have included
	Plenary Investigate the text together, identifying answers to the *wh-* questions. Emphasise to the class that these answers help to make a successful opening.	

DAY 1 ■ Phase 2: Making storyboards

Key features	Stages	Additional opportunities
	Introduction Explain that at the same time as reading an extended story, the children are also going to write their own. Ask them to think about what they will need. (For example: ideas about people in the story and what happens to them.)	**Phonics:** girl **HFW:** boy, girl
Communication: work collaboratively in paired and whole-class contexts	**Speaking and listening** Let partners share ideas on how they should begin planning a story. What do they need to decide? Share ideas as a class. Agree that a story needs four key ingredients: 1. characters; 2. setting; 3. events in a logical sequence, leading to... 4. ending. Display photocopiable page 87 'Mix and match storyboard', which features a collection of settings, characters and key events. Talk about it with the children and demonstrate how they could use it.	
	Independent work Give out copies of photocopiable page 87. Ask the children to discuss in pairs how they would each mix and match pictures to form their own story. Suggest using colours, joining lines, numbers and arrows.	**Extend:** children could create more than one storyboard and choose the best one to take forward
Evaluation: judge the quality of their own work	**Plenary** Let children present their completed storyboards. Did they find them useful? Suggest that the children need their ideas in a written plan.	

DAY 2 ▪ Phase 1: Making a plot summary

Key features	Stages	Additional opportunities
	Introduction Remind the children about the serial you are reading together, *Stanley and the Magic Lamp*.	**Phonics:** w*o*re, h*er* **HFW:** home, brother
Communication: work collaboratively in paired and whole-class contexts	**Speaking and listening** Ask the children to talk to a partner about what happened in the story in the first episode. Share ideas as a class and check by re-reading *Stanley and the Magic Lamp (Part 1)*. Create and save a page entitled *Plot summary*. Explain that this will be the class's ongoing record of key events. Agree on the notes to write for Episode 1. Display and read *Stanley and the Magic Lamp (Part 2)*.	
Communication: communicate outcomes orally and in writing	**Independent work** Invite the children to re-read and discuss Part 2 of the story with a partner. Ask them to write four notes that record the key events of this episode. **Plenary** Listen to the children's notes. Encourage them to recognise that some points are minor and some are key events. Agree on the notes that you will add to the class plot summary.	**Extend:** children can write more than four notes

DAY 2 ▪ Phase 2: Planning the story

Key features	Stages	Additional opportunities
	Introduction Remind the children of the mix and match storyboard they created on Day 1.	**Phonics:** f*oo*t, h*ou*se **HFW:** house, ball
Communication: work collaboratively in paired and whole-class contexts	**Speaking and listening** Ask the children to talk through their board again with a partner. Do their ideas make sense? Do they need to make changes? Bring the class together. Display a copy of photocopiable page 29 'Story planner'. Demonstrate how to use ideas from the mix and match storyboard to make notes under the headings on the planner.	
Self-awareness: learn how to organise their own work	**Independent work** Using their mix and match storyboard as a guide, the children should plan their story in writing on a copy of photocopiable page 29 'Story planner'. Remind them to write clear notes under the headings. **Plenary** Scan the children's completed story planners and display them on the whiteboard so that volunteers can present their plans to the rest of the class.	

DAY 3 ▪ Phase 1: Linking key events

Key features	Stages	Additional opportunities
	Introduction Display and read *Stanley and the Magic Lamp (Part 2)* from the CD-ROM.	**Phonics:** cl*ou*d, m*ore* **HFW:** black, down
	Speaking and listening Ask the children to talk to a partner about what happens in this extract. What is the key event? Share ideas as a class. Agree that it is the appearance of a genie from the teapot. Highlight the important sentence containing the word *genie*.	
Communication: develop their ability to discuss as they work collaboratively in paired contexts	**Independent work** Give the children copies of *Stanley and the Magic Lamp (Part 1)* from the CD-ROM. Ask them to read it and discuss the text with a partner. Can the children identify the key event that links this opening part of the story to the key event in the second extract? Ask them to decide which sentence(s) to highlight.	**Extend:** children can consider how they would have created a link between these two parts of the story
	Plenary Share ideas, agreeing that the link between key events is the teapot that had rolled onto the beach. Display the first extract and identify and highlight this part. Remind the children of the plot summary that you created. Check that both key events have been noted on here. Demonstrate how to link them with an arrow to show how the author has created a logical sequence in the story.	

DAY 3 ▪ Phase 2: A logical sequence

Key features	Stages	Additional opportunities
	Introduction Remind the children that they are planning to write their own extended story. Ask them to look at their written story planner that they created on Phase 2, Day 2. Remind them of the way the author of *Stanley and the Magic Lamp* created links between key events.	**Phonics:** gr*ou*nd, cl*oa*k **HFW:** tree, play
Social skills: listen to and respect other people's ideas	**Speaking and listening** Ask the children to discuss their plans with a partner. Can their partner help them to spot places where key events need linking?	
Self-awareness: learn how to organise their own work	**Independent work** Ask the children to improve their plans so that their key events have a logical sequence. The children may need to change the order of some events or add some new events so that there are links. Suggest that the children use arrows to help them check they have links.	
	Plenary Scan the children's work so that they can present their improved plans to the class on the interactive whiteboard.	

DAY 4 ■ Phase 1: Improvising dialogue

Key features	Stages	Additional opportunities
	Introduction Display and read *Stanley and the Magic Lamp (Part 2)* from the CD-ROM. Point out that the story has stopped at a key moment.	**Phonics:** cl*ou*d, m*o*re **HFW:** his, down
	Speaking and listening Ask the children, working in small groups, to discuss what might happen next.	
Communication: work collaboratively in group contexts	**Independent work** Ask the children, in their groups, to take the parts of the characters and improvise their dialogue after this key event. Encourage them to keep pausing for discussion, considering whether their dialogue has fitted in with the author's earlier writing. Should they change it? They should then try the oral scene again.	**Support:** move between groups and suggest lines of dialogue
	Plenary Ask the children to share their dialogue with the class. Help out by modelling likely dialogue as you take one of the roles yourself.	

DAY 4 ■ Phase 2: A successful story

Key features	Stages	Additional opportunities
	Introduction Remind the children of their plan to write an extended story. Ask: *What do you expect of this type of story? How will it differ from shorter ones?*	**Phonics:** p*ar*k, fl*ew* **HFW:** house, school
Communication: work collaboratively in paired contexts	**Speaking and listening** Encourage the children to discuss with a partner how they will know if their story is successful. What features are important in any extended story? Share ideas as a class.	
Communication: communicate outcomes orally and in writing	**Independent work** The children must ask themselves: *What do I think will make my finished story successful?* Building on their earlier partner discussion, they should make a checklist list of features that will be in their finished story.	
	Plenary Listen to the children's checklists. Point out some of the success criteria that they may have overlooked. In particular, emphasise the logical sequencing of events and the inclusion of the four main parts of a story: opening; something happens; events to sort out; ending.	

DAY 5 ◼ Phase 1: Making predictions

Key features	Stages	Additional opportunities
	Introduction Ask the children if they remember what happened at the end of *Stanley and the Magic Lamp (Part 2)* from the CD-ROM. Discuss how the extract ended.	**Phonics:** *scare, good* **HFW:** then, would
Communication: work collaboratively in paired and whole-class contexts	**Speaking and listening** Let partners exchange ideas on what they predict is going to happen. Will the genie bring happiness? Will anything go wrong? Share ideas as a class. Remind the children of the third part of an extended story: events to sort out. Ask: *Does this mean something bad must happen?*	
	Independent work Ask the children to make a list of events that they think may happen in the rest of the story. In particular, what is the event that will need sorting out?	**Support:** children can make just two predictions
	Plenary Share ideas as a class before you read aloud (from your own book) more of *Stanley and the Magic Lamp.* Try to reach the part where a Liophant appears. How accurate were the predictions? Do the children have any that can be ticked off?	**Extend:** children can talk about textual clues that helped them to make their predictions

DAY 5 ◼ Phase 2: A class checklist

Key features	Stages	Additional opportunities
Evaluation: discuss success criteria for their written work **Communication:** work collaboratively in paired and whole-class contexts	**Introduction** Remind the children of their checklist for an extended story. Work together to create a checklist for success. Include the following points: ■ four main parts of the story ■ a logical sequence of events ■ complete sentences grouped together to tell the different parts of the story ■ the past tense ■ descriptions of character and setting ■ some dialogue. As you write points, supply oral examples from *Stanley and the Magic Lamp.* Save the list. Display and read *Stanley and the Magic Lamp (Part 2).* Point out the dialogue, the grouping of sentences and the use of the past tense.	**Phonics:** *cloud, more* **HFW:** black, down
	Speaking and listening Encourage the children to discuss with their partners whether or not they think events so far in the story show a logical sequence.	**Extend:** one child can mention a key event and the other can say how it is linked to others
Self-awareness: learn how to organise their own work	**Independent work** Ask the children to write a past tense description for another animal arrival – the Kangoceros!	
	Plenary Enjoy the descriptions of the strange new animal.	

DAY 6 ■ Phase 1: All about Stanley

Key features	Stages	Additional opportunities
	Introduction Explain to the class that you are particularly interested in one character from your extended story – Stanley. Read *Stanley and the Magic Lamp (Part 1)* from the CD-ROM. Ask the children: *What do we learn about Stanley?* Draw a large outline of a boy, to represent Stanley, and make a note of your agreed conclusions inside his outline. Display *Stanley and the Magic Lamp (Part 2)*.	**Phonics:** cloud, more **HFW:** his, down
Communication: work collaboratively in paired contexts	**Speaking and listening** Ask the children to read Part 2 of the story with a partner. What new information can they find out about the character of Stanley? Does the writer give clues about how Stanley thinks and feels?	
	Independent work Using photocopiable page 86 'All about Stanley', the children should write three characteristics they have discovered in episodes 1 and 2 of the story. These can be written within the thought bubbles coming from him.	**Extend:** children can add extra thoughts and feelings to the sheet
Communication: communicate outcomes orally	**Speaking and listening** Put the children into pairs with one child taking the role of Stanley and the other, the genie. Stanley has two minutes to introduce himself and explain what sort of person he is to the genie. Then the children should swap roles.	

DAY 6 ■ Phase 2: Story openings

Key features	Stages	Additional opportunities
Evaluation: discuss success criteria for their written work **Communication:** work collaboratively in paired and whole-class contexts	**Introduction** Remind the children of your way of recognising that an extended story has everything it needs. Display the checklist for success you created on Phase 2, Day 5. Add and explain these further success criteria: ■ story language ■ consistent use of the third person ■ temporal connectives to link each part. Display and read *Stanley and the Magic Lamp (Part 1)*. Point out examples of how the author has been careful in his use of the third person.	**Phonics:** main, part **HFW:** four, some
	Speaking and listening Suggest that the children need to remind themselves of their story plans, talking through their story planners with a partner. Then they need to think about a good story opening.	
Self-awareness: learn how to organise their own work	**Independent work** Let the children concentrate on their story opening, rehearsing possibilities orally with their writing group before actually writing. Decide whether the children will write on paper or on screen. Using the computer will allow children to make changes more easily.	**Support:** children can gain confidence by rehearsing openings with a partner before they write
	Plenary Emphasise the value of rehearsing sentences orally, and encourage the children to re-read sentences as they write.	

DAY 7 ■ Phase 1: Going through changes

Key features	Stages	Additional opportunities
	### Introduction Remind the children of your special interest in the Stanley character from your extended story. Use the children's character studies from Phase 1, Day 6 to revise what you have discovered so far. Read out the text from the book that describes the Liophant's arrival.	**Phonics:** sn*o*rt, g*oo*d **HFW:** your, what
Communication: work collaboratively in paired contexts	### Speaking and listening Ask: *What do we learn here about Stanley? How is he feeling now?* Encourage the children to discuss these questions with their partners.	
	### Independent work After re-reading their work from Phase 1, Day 6, the children should write a new set of notes, thoughts or speech bubbles. Emphasise the need to recognise what the author is telling the reader about Stanley's thoughts.	**Extend:** children can add extra thoughts and feelings to the sheet
Communication: develop their ability to discuss	### Plenary Remind the children that characters change during the course of a story. Discuss the changes that the children could predict will take place for the character of Stanley.	

DAY 7 ■ Phase 2: A work in progress

Key features	Stages	Additional opportunities
	### Introduction Remind the children that they are writing or have written their story opening. Talk about the value of making connections. How will they link what they have written to what comes next? Do they need a time connective? Make a class list of connectives that the children may find useful. (For example: *Just then...; Right away...; As soon as...*)	**Phonics:** t*i*me, s*oo*n **HFW:** as, then
	### Speaking and listening Ask the children to talk to a partner about where they are up to in their story. Are they planning to use a connective soon?	
Self-awareness: maintain their concentration to complete a polished story	### Independent work Suggest that the children get back to being authors by re-reading what they have already written. What does their plan tell them comes next? Emphasise that authors do not get it right first time! The children should think of their story as a work in progress. Sitting in small writing groups will help, with children composing their sentences, rehearsing them orally, re-reading and checking as they are writing.	**Support:** work closely with children who find writing difficult
Evaluation: judge the quality of their own writing	### Plenary Discuss the children's progress. Would anyone like to read their opening sentence to the rest of the class?	

DAY 8 ◢ Phase 1: Conversation clues

Key features	Stages	Additional opportunities
	Introduction Read out the text from the book about the Liophant's arrival. Point out the early dialogue between Stanley and the genie.	**Phonics:** sn*o*rt, g*oo*d **HFW:** your, what
Communication: work collaboratively in paired, group and whole-class contexts	**Speaking and listening** Ask the children to discuss with their partners why they think that this dialogue is important. Share ideas as a class. Talk about how the reader learns that Stanley does not like fierce animals, only friendly ones. Ask the children: *What about the story's plot? How does this dialogue move the story on?* (It brings in the problem of a large animal.)	
Social skills: listen to and respect other people's ideas	**Independent work** Ask the children, in pairs or groups of three, to read the dialogue only in this extract. They need to share ideas on how the conversation could continue. Suggest that Arthur could become involved.	**Support:** ask your teaching assistant to suggest to the children some dialogue that Arthur might say
	Plenary Listen to the children's ideas, perhaps making suggestions of your own.	

DAY 8 ◢ Phase 2: Including dialogue

Key features	Stages	Additional opportunities
	Introduction Remind the children that dialogue can be a useful way of moving the story along. Display and read *Stanley and the Magic Lamp (Part 1)* from the CD-ROM. Highlight the dialogue. Ask the class: *What does the dialogue tell us about the characters?* Point out how the speech is set out and the link verb that is used: *said* in all three cases.	**Phonics:** sp*ee*ch **HFW:** said, what
	Speaking and listening Give partners two minutes to discuss alternatives to *said*. Share ideas as you experiment with some on the board.	
Self-awareness: maintain their concentration to complete a polished story	**Independent work** In their writing groups, let the children continue with their stories. Remind them to keep the practice of composing their sentences, rehearsing them orally with a partner, re-reading and checking as they are writing. Remind them to include some dialogue in their story.	**Support:** give the children a list of link verbs to use with their dialogue
Evaluation: judge the quality of their own writing	**Plenary** Discuss problems that the children are encountering. Do they find their plans useful? Is it helpful to speak words before writing them?	

DAY 9 ▪ Phase 1: Acting out a scene

Key features	Stages	Additional opportunities
	### Introduction Again, begin the lesson by reading the text about the Liophant's arrival to the children. Remind them that you are focusing on dialogue. Ask: *Why has the author sometimes used dialogue? Does it bring the story to life?* Remind the children that some dialogue was on their story checklist. Do the children think that this story has a good balance of prose description and dialogue?	**Phonics:** sn*o*rt, g*oo*d **HFW:** your, what
Communication: work collaboratively in paired and group contexts	### Speaking and listening Children can work in the dialogue pairs or small groups from Phase 1, Day 8. Ask them to discuss what they were doing.	
Communication: communicate outcomes orally	### Independent work Set the task of acting out this extract of the book. The children will need to add to the author's dialogue, as they extend the conversation beyond the end of it. Arthur could also be involved. Ask them to rehearse their plays, reminding them to use clear speech and appropriate intonation.	**Support:** less confident children will prefer a smaller audience – another pair or group
	### Plenary Give everyone the opportunity to enact their dialogue for an audience. Highlight examples that reveal interesting character development.	

DAY 9 ▪ Phase 2: Joining sentences

Key features	Stages	Additional opportunities
	### Introduction Orally, present the children with two ideas. For example: 1. Stanley liked animals. 2. He wished for one.	**Phonics:** w*o*re, y*ear* **HFW:** brother, home
Self-awareness: maintain their concentration to complete a polished story	### Speaking and listening Working with a partner, ask the children to try out, orally, ways to connect these two sentences. Which connective works best? Write the sentences on the whiteboard, then share ideas as a class and write them as one sentence linked by a connective. Use other examples sentences as you explore different ways to combine more than one idea in a sentence. Display *Stanley and the Magic Lamp (Part 1)* from the CD-ROM. In the opening paragraph, investigate the number of ideas contained in a sentence, and how ideas have been combined with connectives (*since, as*).	
	### Independent work Ask the children to continue with their stories in their writing groups. Remind them to be on the lookout for sentences that would benefit from being joined. Review the children's writing and offer support as necessary by joining and working with different writing groups.	**Support:** give individual advice about pairs of sentences to join
Communication: communicate outcomes orally	### Plenary Listen to the opening paragraphs of some stories. Encourage the children to comment on words or sentences that catch their interest.	

DAY 10 — Phase 1: Marks out of ten

Key features	Stages	Additional opportunities
	Introduction Display and read aloud the final five pages of the *Stanley and the Magic Lamp* book. Ask the children: *Are you satisfied with the ending?* Return to the children's prediction sheets from Phase 1, Day 5. Can any more predictions be ticked off? Did any more come true?	**Phonics:** head, yawned **HFW:** when, night
Communication: work collaboratively in paired, group and whole-class contexts	**Speaking and listening** Remind the children about the class checklist for a successful extended story. Encourage them to work with their partners and remember as many points on the list as they can. Share results as a class and refer back to the checklist for success you created on Phase 2, Days 5 and 6.	
	Independent work Ask the children to mark *Stanley and the Magic Lamp* against the checklist for sucess. How many marks out of ten does this book receive for each feature on the list? What is the total mark?	**Support:** children can work with a partner
Communication: communicate outcomes orally	**Plenary** Compare results in small discussion groups and then as a class. What is the average score?	

DAY 10 — Phase 2: Linking story sections

Key features	Stages	Additional opportunities
	Introduction Perform two actions for the children. Then ask: *What did I do?* On the board, write the answers in two sentences. For example: a. *I put on my glasses.* b. *I switched on the computer.*	**Phonics:** yawn, good **HFW:** night, boy
Communication: work collaboratively in group and whole-class contexts	**Speaking and listening** Ask the children to discuss with their partners how they could combine the two ideas into one sentence. As a class, discuss temporal connectives. For example: *before, after, while.* Demonstrate how to compose sentences with subordination for time and reason. For example: *The boy rushed in as soon as the bell rang.* Explain that temporal connectives (phrases or words) are an important way to make sections of an extended story hang together. Point out: *Almost a year had passed,* at the start of *Stanley and the Magic Lamp (Part 1)* from the CD-ROM. Read aloud the final pages of the book. Discuss why it makes a good ending to the story.	
Self-awareness: maintain their concentration to complete a polished story	**Independent work** Suggest that the children check with their writing groups that they have enough temporal connectives in their stories. As they reach the final section, they need to think how they will link it to the preceding section(s). Emphasise that they should be following plans, rehearsing sentences, re-reading and checking.	**Support:** give the children a list of suggested connectives
Communication: communicate outcomes orally	**Plenary** Practise using temporal connectives in oral work.	

DAY 11 ▪ Phase 1: Evaluating the story

Key features	Stages	Additional opportunities
	Introduction Read the children a review of an appropriate fiction book – Scholastic's *Child Education* magazine has good examples. Point out that before recommending this book, the reviewer checked that: ■ the book's plot was complicated enough ■ there was sufficient character detail ■ the author sustained the reader's interest. From one of your class stories, read the final page of a section that finishes on a cliffhanger.	**Phonics:** read, part **HFW:** good, what
Communication: work collaboratively in paired, group and whole-class contexts	**Speaking and listening** Ask the children to discuss with their partners: *What has just happened? Does it make you want to read on?* Bring the class together and introduce the term *cliffhanger.* Suggest that it is an effective technique for ending one part of an extended story because the reader will stay interested.	
	Independent work Ask the children to evaluate *Stanley and the Magic Lamp.* Checking as before against the class checklist for success (Phase 2, Days 5 and 6), would the *Child Education* book reviewer include it on his or her page?	
	Plenary Create reading groups so the children can discuss the story and compare their evaluations.	

DAY 11 ▪ Phase 2: Success criteria

Key features	Stages	Additional opportunities
	Introduction Remind the children of the criteria you agreed as a class for writing a successful story (Phase 2, Days 5 and 6).	**Phonics:** part **HFW:** some, four
Evaluation: discuss success criteria for their written work, and judge the quality of their own writing	**Speaking and listening** Ask the children to work with a partner and discuss points from the list. How many can they remember? Bring the class together and display the checklist for success.	
Self-awareness: maintain their concentration to complete a polished story	**Independent work** Working in their writing groups, ask the children to check that their stories are finished. They then need to review their own completed work, using the checklist. Does anything need changing in their story? Can they make any improvements? **Plenary** Talk about the class's checklist for success. Which points have proved difficult to include?	

DAY 12 ▪ Phase 1: Reading clubs

Key features	Stages	Additional opportunities
Communication: develop their ability to discuss as they work collaboratively in group contexts	**Introduction** Put out sets of longer stories that the children can read independently. Support children in their selections, suggesting that they get into groups and form reading clubs. Give each club member a copy of the same book. Explain that club members will all read up to a certain point before they pause for discussion. **Speaking and listening** Club members should debate and decide on good stopping points. **Independent work** Let the reading clubs read, waiting for each member to reach the planned point and then discussing the story so far. Remind them to discuss the book's plot and characters, and how it holds the reader's interest. **Plenary** Ask clubs and individuals to comment on the books they have read. Would they recommend them on the magazine book review page? (Phase 1, Day 11) Why?	**Phonics:** book, read **Support:** children should read with children of similar competence **Extend:** children should read with children of similar competence, perhaps moving to a second book

DAY 12 ▪ Phase 2: Improving presentation

Key features	Stages	Additional opportunities
	Introduction Hold up a book, an extended story such as *Stanley and the Magic Lamp*. Ask the children: *What helps to improve its presentation?* Suggest that appealing presentation is important if other members of the class (or a parallel class) are going to want to read the children's stories. Talk about the benefits of reading on paper or on screen.	**Phonics:** screen, read **HFW:** what, your
Communication: communicate outcomes in writing and through ICT	**Speaking and listening** Encourage the children to debate the value of illustrations with their partner or writing group. Would illustrations improve their stories? Which parts? Bring the class together and show them how illustrations have been used effectively in your extended story.	**Support:** provide computer support if needed
Self-awareness: maintain their concentration to complete a polished story	**Independent work** Let the children make presentational changes to their finished story. **Plenary** Hold a celebration as the children read one another's stories.	

Guided writing
As a class, write a plan for a new story featuring Stanley and Arthur. Divide the story into sections for the children to write up. Encourage them to refer back to the original story to make sure that the characters act and speak appropriately.

Assessment
Ask the children to write a review of *Stanley and the Magic Lamp*, explaining how well they think it meets your class's success criteria. Refer back to the learning outcomes on page 71.

Further work
Encourage the children to continue with their reading clubs, and to evaluate – either orally or in writing – each book they read.

DAY 1 ▪ Dramatising key moments

Key features	Stages	Additional opportunities
	Introduction Remind the children of how they enacted a key moment in *Stanley and the Magic Lamp* (Phase 1, Day 4). Ask them: *What about the extended stories you have written? What are the key moments?*	**Phonics:** note, freeze
Communication: work collaboratively in group contexts	**Speaking and listening** Put the children into groups of about four to compare the key moments of their stories. They must choose a key moment to use as the basis for a dramatised presentation. (Move among the groups, making sure that they choose wisely.)	
Communication: communicate outcomes orally	**Independent work** The children must prepare their dramatisations. They need to decide whereabouts in the dramatisation the key moment will come: at the beginning, during the scene, or as the final climax. Children need to allocate the different parts, and decide who will say what and when. Remind the children that they will probably need to make play production notes. Suggest that they improvise most of their dialogue.	**Support:** make sure that children have a role they feel comfortable with
	Plenary Ask for progress updates. The children should keep their notes for tomorrow.	

DAY 2 ▪ Beginning rehearsals

Key features	Stages	Additional opportunities
	Introduction Remind the children about their production notes. Today they must begin rehearsals! Point out that the dramatisation should emphasise the key moment of the story.	**Phonics:** note, speech
Communication: work collaboratively in group contexts	**Speaking and listening** Re-form groups and ask the children to remind themselves of their current stage of progress.	
Communication: communicate outcomes orally	**Independent work** Allow space for rehearsals. Move among groups, offering help and advice. Encourage the children to pause during rehearsals if they realise something is not right, and then try that part again. Remind them about the importance of clear speech and appropriate intonation, as well as appropriate body language.	
	Plenary Admit that you have taken a peek at the groups' rehearsals. In turn, ask the groups to freeze-frame a moment from their rehearsals so the rest of the class can see as well.	

DAY 3 ■ What a performance!

Key features	Stages	Additional opportunities
	Introduction Tell the children that today is performance day! Provide everyone with a copy of photocopiable page 88 'Theatre critic'.	**Phonics:** *how, high* **HFW:** *how*
	Speaking and listening Let groups present their dramatisations.	
Communication: communicate outcomes orally and in writing	**Independent work** After each presentation, ask the theatre critics in the audience to make two notes on photocopiable page 88: ■ what they thought the highlight of the presentation was ■ suggestions, as to how and where they, if they were the director, would make improvements.	**Support:** children can write with a partner
Evaluation: give feedback to others	**Plenary** Model how to make constructive criticism by providing your review of the performances. Ask the children for their reviews. Did many children identify a key moment as their highlight?	

Guided reading

Provide the children with an extended story to read in groups with your teaching assistant. Ask them to discuss the story together and identify the key moments together.

Assessment

Use the 'Label the story' interactive assessment activity from the CD-ROM. Read the story with the children and read the drag-and-drop labels.
Ask the children to decide where each label should be dragged and dropped into place.
Refer back to the learning outcomes on page 71.

Further work

Ask the children to extend the assessment task by writing their own short story and then choosing the correct place to drag and drop each label.

All about Stanley

NARRATIVE ■ UNIT 4

Episode 1

Episode 2

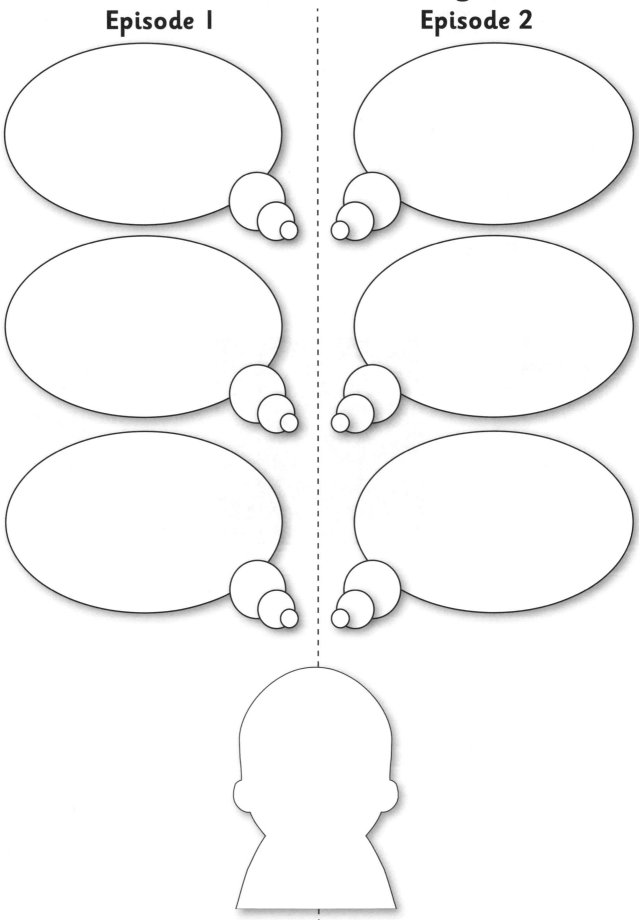

PHOTOCOPIABLE

SCHOLASTIC
www.scholastic.co.uk

Mix and match storyboard

   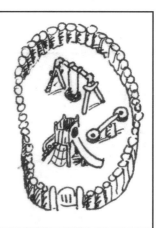

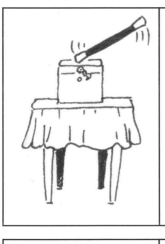 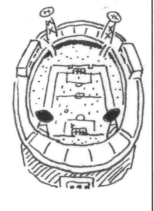  

Illustration © Neil Chapman/Beehive Illustration.

Name ———————————————— **Date** ————————————————

Theatre critic

■ Use this sheet to make notes about each presentation.

Group	Highlight	How to improve

100 LITERACY FRAMEWORK LESSONS YEAR 2

PHOTOCOPIABLE ■SCHOLASTIC
www.scholastic.co.uk

NON-FICTION
UNIT 1 Instructions

Speak and listen for a range of purposes on paper and on screen

Strand 1 Speaking
■ Speak with clarity and use appropriate intonation when reading and reciting texts.
Strand 2 Listening and responding
■ Listen to others in class, ask relevant questions and follow instructions.
Strand 3 Group discussion and interaction
■ Ensure that everyone contributes, allocate tasks, and consider alternatives and reach agreement.

Read for a range of purposes on paper and on screen

Strand 5 Word recognition: decoding (reading) and encoding (spelling)
■ Read independently and with increasing fluency longer and less familiar texts.
■ Spell with increasing accuracy and confidence, drawing on word recognition and knowledge of word structure and spelling patterns.
■ Know how to tackle unfamiliar words which are not completely decodable.
■ Read and spell less common alternative graphemes including trigraphs.
■ Read high and medium frequency words independently and automatically.
Strand 6 Word structure and spelling
■ Spell with increasing accuracy and confidence, drawing on word recognition and knowledge of word structure and spelling patterns including common inflections and use of double letters.
■ Read and spell less common alternative graphemes including trigraphs.
Strand 7 Understanding and interpreting texts
■ Draw together ideas and information from across a whole text, using simple signposts in the text.
■ Explain organisational features of texts, including alphabetical order, layout, diagrams, captions, hyperlinks and bullet points.
Strand 8 Engaging with and responding to texts
■ Engage with books through exploring and enacting interpretations.

Write for a range of purposes on paper and on screen

Strand 9 Creating and shaping texts
■ Draw on knowledge and experience of texts in deciding and planning what and how to write.
■ Maintain consistency in non-narrative, including purpose and tense.
■ Select from different presentational features to suit particular writing purposes on paper and on screen.
Strand 10 Text structure and organisation
■ Use appropriate language to make sections hang together.
Strand 11 Sentence structure and punctuation
■ Use question marks and use commas to separate items in a list.

Progression in instructional texts

In this year, children are moving towards:
■ Listening to and following a series of more complex instructions.
■ Giving clear oral instructions to members of a group.

▶

UNIT 1 ◄ **Instructions** *continued*

■ Reading and following simple sets of instructions such as recipes, plans and constructions which include diagrams.
■ Analysing some instructional texts and noting their function, form and typical language features.
■ As part of a group with the teacher, composing a set of instructions with additional diagrams. Write simple instructions independently, for example getting to school, playing a game.

Key aspects of learning covered in this Unit

Enquiry
Children will ask questions arising from work in another area of the curriculum, for example questions about planting beans.
Reasoning
Children will sequence actions logically to form a set of instructions.
Evaluation
Children will give instructions orally and in writing. They will judge the effectiveness of their own work.
Social skills
When working collaboratively children will learn about listening to and respecting other people's contributions.
Communication
Children will develop their ability to discuss as they work collaboratively in paired, group and whole-class contexts. They will communicate outcomes orally, in writing and through ICT if appropriate.

Prior learning

Before starting this Unit check that the children can:
■ Listen to and follow at least three consecutive instructions.
■ Read and follow simple written instructions.
If they need further support please refer to a prior Unit or a similar Unit in Year 1.

Resources

Sequence 1, Phase 1:
Photocopiable page 104 'How to make a Chinese New Year Lantern'; Tape recorder
Sequence 1, Phase 2:
Photocopiable page 105 'How to act in our classroom'
Sequence 1, Phase 3:
Photocopiable page 106 'Checklist for instructions'
Sequence 2, Phase 1:
How to grow beans by Eileen Jones ❀; *How to make an ice cream cornet* by Eileen Jones ❀; Photocopiable page 105 'How to act in our classroom'
Sequence 2, Phase 2:
Photocopiable page 105 'How to act in our classroom'
Sequence 2, Phase 3:
Instruction skeleton ❀; Assessment activity 'Writing instructions' ❀

Cross-curricular opportunities

PE – Games activities.
Science – Green plants.
PSHE – Taking and sharing responsibility.

UNIT 1 ■ Teaching sequence 1

Phase	Children's objectives	Summary of activities	Learning outcomes
1	I can listen to and follow instructions. I can work with a group to create oral instructions for a new game. I can test and give oral instructions.	Listen to and follow instructions for a new PE activity Arrange instructions in the correct order. Give oral instructions for a group PE activity	Children can follow a series of simple instructions. Children can effectively give oral instructions in the correct sequence.
2	I can give instructions in two ways – by giving an order and by describing the process. I can give instructions orally and in writing.	Play a 'Simon says...' game. Use two oral ways of giving instructions. Write instructions in two ways.	Children can say and write instructions in two forms.
3	I can give clear instructions. I can follow instructions. I can improve my instructions. I can write a checklist to help other people to write instructions.	Rehearse oral instructions for a familiar procedure. Test oral instructions on a partner. Contribute to modelled writing for instructions for the procedure. Agree on instructions to add to the instructions. Develop a checklist for effective instructions.	Children can say and write a simple sequence of instructions to be followed by another child.

UNIT 1 ■ Teaching sequence 2

Phase	Children's objectives	Summary of activities	Learning outcomes
1	I can discuss and follow different types of instructions. I can identify what makes instructions easier to follow. I understand how diagrams are used with instructions.	Read and follow instructions in groups. Identify how to make instruction texts easier to follow. Compare form and structure of instruction texts.	Children can read and follow a simple sequence of instructions related to another curriculum area or classroom procedure. Children can identify key features of written instructions.
2	I can identify how instructions can be improved. I can discuss and agree on diagrams to include. I can use organisational features to make instructions clearer.	Edit the wording of a class instruction text Plan diagrams to support text. Finalise layout of text.	Children can write a series of instructions, including diagrams.
3	I can plan instructions. I can test my instructions. I can edit my instructions. I can include sequence words and diagrams.	Plan independent writing. Use a checklist for independent writing. Complete writing and add diagrams. Evaluate the success of the instructions.	Children can write a simple sequence of instructions to be followed by another child or group. Children can use appropriate tense consistently, indicate sequence clearly, for example through numbering or use of sequencing words, and include a detailed diagram.

Provide copies of the objectives for the children.

DAY 1 ■ Listening to instructions

Key features	Stages	Additional opportunities
	Introduction Give the children plenty of space, perhaps working in the hall. Explain that you are going to teach them a short, warm-up game for PE.	**Phonics:** *each,* blow **HFW:** ball, then
	Speaking and listening Encourage the children to concentrate carefully as you begin to give your instructions. For example: *Choose a partner. Place a ball between you.* Gradually build up the number of instructions as the game proceeds. For example: *Find a space and stand facing each other.*	
Enquiry: ask questions arising from work in another area of the curriculum **Communication:** work collaboratively in paired, group and whole-class contexts	**Independent work** Encourage the children to ask questions about sequence and detail as your instructions mount up. For example: *Roll the ball to each other until my whistle blows. Then link up with another pair. After that, you must....* Have another run through as you make a tape recording of your final version of the instructions. (Two minutes will be long enough.) Make a point of leaving out some key language features (such as regular use of imperatives) for editing later. **Plenary** Play the tape again as the children follow the instructions. Point out that familiarity has given them confidence.	**Support:** use demonstration to guide children

DAY 2 ■ A logical sequence

Key features	Stages	Additional opportunities
	Introduction Let the children listen to and follow your taped instructions from yesterday. Ask them: *Did the order of my instructions matter?* Agree on the need for a logical sequence.	**Phonics:** short, clear **HFW:** more, what
Reasoning: sequence actions logically to form a set of instructions	**Independent work** Put the children into pairs. Give out scissors, paper, glue and copies of photocopiable page 104 'How to make a Chinese New Year lantern'. Suggest that these instructions are in the wrong order. The children should cut out the sections, sort them into a logical sequence, and then stick them on to paper. **Plenary** Compare the results. Discuss what helped the children. Ask: *Did you use the sentence starting words? How did they help you?* Plan to put the instructions to the test at Chinese New Year.	

DAY 3 ■ Developing new instructions

Key features	Stages	Additional opportunities
	Introduction Return to Day 1's PE exercise. Play the tape of instructions and explain that you need more short, warm-up games for your PE lessons.	**Phonics:** short, clear **HFW:** more, what
Evaluation: give instructions orally **Social skills:** listen to and respect other people's contributions	**Independent work** Put the children into groups of about four and ask each group to develop a game. Encourage everyone in the group to be involved in talking about equipment and instructions that will be needed in their game. Stress the need for a clear sequence, otherwise the game will not work. Suggest they practise on themselves, taking turns to say the instructions as the others try them out. Do they need to revise the instructions or change the sequence? Move from group to group making tape recordings and ask your teaching assistant to do the same. When the groups are ready, suggest they try out their instructions on another group.	**Support:** offer to help with sequencing
Evaluation: judge the effectiveness of their own work	**Plenary** Play the recordings and ask the rest of the class to try out the games. Ask: *Which instructions were clearest? Which ones did you follow easily?*	

Guided writing

Working in the same groups as before, ask the children to talk through their PE exercise as your teaching assistant models how to write each instruction. Encourage the groups to review their work and decide if their instructions are clear.

Assessment

Play your taped instructions again. Assess how accurately the children follow the instructions.
Give the children instructions for a class activity, such as a game of I-Spy. Deliberately give your four instructions in the wrong sequence. Can the children tell you the correct sequence?
Refer back to the learning outcomes on page 91.

Further work

Ask the children to think of a game they have played at home or in the playground.
They must teach this game to someone else.
Suggest they work out a sequence of clear instructions.
Allow them to test and evaluate the instructions.

DAY 1 ▨ Simon says...

Key features	Stages	Additional opportunities
	Introduction Tell the children that it's time for a game! Explain that your game is similar to 'Simon says....' The rule of your game is: Do exactly and only what you are told. Demonstrate by giving the children a few instructions involving simple actions for them to obey. For example: *Nod your head; Tap your fingers.*	**Phonics:** *rule, game* **HFW:** do, your, play
Evaluation: give instructions orally **Communication:** work collaboratively in paired contexts	**Independent work** Ask the children to continue to play the game with their partners. Encourage them to keep to instructions for simple procedures, for example, coming into the room and sitting down. **Plenary** Give practise in giving and following instructions as children take your place and tell everyone what to do.	

DAY 2 ▨ Instruct and obey

Key features	Stages	Additional opportunities
	Introduction Remind the children of yesterday's partner game. Model it again, this time using language in two ways: ■ First by giving an order: *Open the door.* ■ Then by describing the process: *First you open the door.* Repeat this double approach with another example: ■ *Walk through the gap.* ■ *Then you walk through the gap.*	**Phonics:** *door* **HFW:** door, you
Evaluation: give instructions orally	**Speaking and listening** Let the children work out a pair of examples with their partners before you share them as a class.	
Communication: work collaboratively in paired contexts	**Independent work** Ask the children, in pairs, to continue giving instructions to each other. Suggest that the game now has an additional rule: ■ Do exactly and only what you are told. ■ Only do what you are told if the instructions are given in two different ways.	**Support:** work with pairs of children to ensure they understand the difference between the two types of instructions
Evaluation: judge the effectiveness of their own work	**Plenary** Let the class listen and watch as pairs of children instruct and obey. Encourage others to suggest language changes where necessary.	

DAY 3 ■ Using imperatives

Key features	Stages	Additional opportunities
	### Introduction Ask the children: *Who can remember a pair of their instructions from yesterday?* Let a volunteer say them as the rest of the class does as they are told. Write a pair of instructions on the whiteboard: ■ *Hold up a book.* ■ *First you hold up a book.* Compare the language features of the two. What do the children notice? Highlight the word *you* in the second version. Ask: *Is* you *used in the first version?* Highlight *Hold* in the first sentence. Explain that the verb *hold* is in an imperative form here and can give the instruction without the word *you*.	**Phonics:** first **HFW:** you, do
Evaluation: give instructions orally and in writing	### Speaking and listening Let the children practise giving instructions both ways with their partners. ### Independent work Ask the children to write pairs of instructions linked to body movements: one with an imperative verb, one beginning with *First* and using *you*. Suggest they choose a name, perhaps their own, to show that they – not Simon – are telling everyone what to do. ### Plenary Let individuals read out their instructions. Does everyone obey?	**Support:** children can tell a sentence to an adult before writing it **Extend:** children can add additional pairs of sentences

Guided reading

Working with your teaching assistant, ask the children to take turns reading out instructions from photocopiable page 105 'How to act in our classroom'.
Suggest they pause after each text to discuss if the rest of the group understands what to do.
Can the group agree on instructions they would like to see for your classroom?

Assessment

Say a simple sentence beginning with an imperative.
Ask the children to tell you an alternative way to say this, beginning with a connective indicating the sequence of events (*First, Next, Then*). Reverse the process.
Ask the children to provide examples of their own in sentences about making a paper fan or a card.
Refer back to the learning outcomes on page 91.

Further work

List connectives you have been using (*First, Next, Then*).
Ask the children to create sentences, using each of the connectives.
Let them write their sentences about how to make a paper fan, each time expressing their sentence in an alternative way.

DAY 1 ■ Making a folding book

Key features	Stages	Additional opportunities
	Introduction Make sure that the children are familiar with how to make simple folding books, perhaps when writing the story of Florence Nightingale or the Great Fire of London in history. Remind the children about this history work.	**Phonics:** book, fold **HFW:** you, make
Communication: work collaboratively in paired and whole-class contexts	**Speaking and listening** Suggest that the children explain to their partners how they folded their paper to make their book. Bring the class together as you demonstrate and describe how you usually make a folding book.	
Reasoning: sequence actions logically to form a set of instructions	**Independent work** Let the children imagine that a child in another Year 2 class does not know how to make a folding book. The children need to work out clear oral instructions to give. Suggest that they fold a piece of paper as they say their instructions to themselves.	**Support:** children can work with an adult or partner
	Plenary Encourage the children to practise giving oral instructions by demonstrating another simple classroom procedure – for example, saving and closing a computer file or using an interactive whiteboard tool. Ask individual children to give oral instructions for the procedure. Do the instructions work?	

DAY 2 ■ Testing the instructions

Key features	Stages	Additional opportunities
	Introduction Remind the children about yesterday's work. Ask them to rehearse their oral instructions for making a folding book independently.	**Phonics:** book, fold **HFW:** you, make
Evaluation: give instructions orally **Communication:** work collaboratively in paired and whole-class contexts	**Independent work** Put the children into pairs and give each child an appropriate piece of paper for making a folding book. Each partner must take a turn being the instructor, while the other is the guinea pig who follows the instructions. Encourage partners to help each other by pointing out when the instructor's oral instruction is not clear.	
	Plenary Share the children's results and invite them to talk about the difficulties they found following the instructions they were given. How did the instructors improve those instructions?	

DAY 3 ▪ Adding diagrams

Key features	Stages	Additional opportunities
	Introduction Return to yesterday's work. Ask the children: *What changes did you make to your instructions?* Progressing from oral experience, encourage the children to contribute as you model how to write folding book instructions.	**Phonics:** book, fold **HFW:** you, make
Communication: work collaboratively in paired, group and whole-class contexts	**Speaking and listening** Ask: *Would diagrams make these instructions clearer?* Encourage the children to discuss the answer with their partners and then share opinions as a class. **Independent work** Put the children into small groups to consider what diagrams are needed and what they should look like. Bring the children together into groups of six and ask them to share their ideas more widely. Encourage the children to compromise and reach agreement. **Plenary** Collect and discuss ideas from the groups. Help the children to come to a class decision on which diagrams you will need, and add these to the text.	

DAY 4 ▪ A checklist for instructions

Key features	Stages	Additional opportunities
	Introduction Review what the children have learned so far about instructions. Display yesterday's modelled writing and instructions.	**Phonics:** verb, order **HFW:** for, then
Communication: work collaboratively in paired and whole-class contexts **Communication:** communicate outcomes in writing	**Speaking and listening** Let the children exchange views with their partners. Ask: *Are the instructions clear? Could they be improved?* Share opinions as a class, making changes if necessary. **Independent work** Suggest that a checklist would be a helpful guide to someone writing instructions. Ask the children to write a short checklist for writing effective instructions or use photocopiable page 106 'Checklist for instructions'. **Plenary** Share ideas and agree on your class checklist. Include in the list: the purpose of the instructions; requirements; a clear sequence; appropriate verb tense; a detailed diagram.	

Guided reading

Read your modelled writing together.
Ask the children to identify some features that are important for written instructions. Can the children pick out the important verbs?
Guide the children to awareness of an imperative verb's typical position early in the sentence.

Assessment

Explain how to write a set of instructions for a classroom procedure, such as:

■ How to sharpen a pencil
■ How to write on a computer screen
■ How to clear up at home-time.
Refer back to the learning outcomes on page 91.

Further work

Encourage the children to name different ways of indicating sequence clearly. For example: by using numbering or sequencing words.
Have they seen helpful features on a computer? Do they know how to use them? (For example: bullet points.)

DAY 1 ▪ Classroom notices

Key features	Stages	Additional opportunities
	Introduction Make sure before the lesson that your classroom notices include examples of instructions.	**Phonics:** *chair*, *hear* **HFW:** *your*, *down*
Communication: work collaboratively in paired and group contexts	**Speaking and listening** Working with their partners, ask the children to identify an instruction on your classroom walls. Bring the class together and compare results. Display and read photocopiable page 105 'How to act in our classroom'. Explain that these are the instructions for what children should do in this class.	
	Independent work Copy the photocopiable sheet and cut the copies into four separate texts. Put the children into pairs or small groups and give each group one text. The children must discuss and follow the instructions. Move groups to a new text as they finish following their instructions.	
	Plenary Point out a set of instructions on your classroom wall. Ask the children to demonstrate how to follow them.	

DAY 2 ▪ Which is easier to follow?

Key features	Stages	Additional opportunities
	Introduction Return to the classroom instructions from yesterday. Put the children into the same groups.	**Phonics:** *chair*, *hear* **HFW:** *your*, *down*
Communication: work collaboratively in group contexts	**Speaking and listening** Let the groups finish following the four sets of classroom instructions from the photocopiable page. They should then discuss them in their groups. Did they each find all of the instructions equally easy to follow?	
	Independent work Ask the children to identify, independently or in their groups, one of the four sets of instructions that was hard to follow and one that was easier. They need to decide why one was easier to follow than the other.	
	Plenary Display the four texts on the whiteboard. Suggest that the whole point of instructions is that they are easy to follow. Ask the children to give each text a score out of ten, according to how easy it is to follow. They can write and display the score on their individual whiteboards. Compare the results. Discuss why some sets of instructions are clearer than others.	

DAY 3 ■ Using diagrams and hyperlinks

Key features	Stages	Additional opportunities
Enquiry: ask questions arising from another area of the curriculum	**Introduction** Remind the children about the 'How to act in our classroom' instructions on photocopiable page 105. Revise the reasons why some were easier follow than others. How helpful were the diagrams? Display *How to grow beans* and *How to make an ice cream cornet* from the CD-ROM. Ask the children: *What are these instructions for? Which lines tell you?* (The titles.)	**Phonics:** *how, leave* **HFW:** *little, then*
	Speaking and listening Encourage the children to talk about the titles with their partners. Ask: *Are they helpful? What is their job?* Share ideas as a class.	
	Independent work Ask for a comparison between the two texts and invite the children to list similarities in and differences between the form and structure of the two texts. Children may work independently or with a partner.	**Support:** children can work with a partner
Communication: develop their ability to discuss	**Plenary** Compare results. Highlight the similarities and differences that the children mention. Make sure you point out: layout; the way instruction sequence is shown; numbers; bullet points; diagrams; fonts; titles and subtitles. Talk about electronic instruction texts on the internet that contain hyperlinks. Show the children the home page of Scholastic's website: www.scholastic.co.uk Look for the 'Scholastic magazines' section and click on 'Free downloads'. Follow the hyperlinks that link to diagrams.	**Extend:** children can investigate electronic instruction techniques

Guided writing

Read photocopiable page 105 'How to act in our classroom' with the children. Let them discuss adding a new line in each text. What would it say? Where would it be placed? Let the children discuss with a partner and then the group if they think it is an appropriate instruction line.

Assessment

Ask the children to suggest changes in the form and structure of the 'How to act in our classroom' texts.
Ask them:
What would make the instructions easier to understand?
How could they be set out more clearly?
Can you describe some changes you would make to one of the texts?
What diagrams would you add?
Refer back to the learning outcomes on page 91.

Further work

Let the children identify a set of instructions in your classroom that they think they can improve.
Suggest they create a new form and structure to improve it. How should it be set out? Are language additions needed? Would a diagram help?

LIVERPOOL JOHN MOORES UNIVERSITY
LEARNING SERVICES

DAY 1 ■ Improving texts

Key features	Stages	Additional opportunities
Enquiry: ask questions arising from work in another area of the curriculum	### Introduction Before the lesson, check that you have the recording of your PE game instructions from the beginning of this Unit. Make sure that your taped instructions include some inconsistencies of tense and inappropriate use of adverbs or adjectives; if necessary, amend the recording. Remind the children about the game and play the recording. Transcribe the words to the board. Explain that you are going to print these instructions and give them to the class to improve.	**Phonics:** *each*, bl*ow* **HFW:** ball, then
Communication: work collaboratively in paired and whole-class contexts	### Speaking and listening In partner discussion, let the children share opinions on the language of your instructions. Are the sentences as clear as they need to be?	
	### Independent work Ask the children, independently or in pairs, to list faults that they find with the language of the instructions.	**Support:** draw the children's attention to the different features of the text, such as the tenses
	### Plenary Share the children's ideas. (For example: sentences may be too long; have too many unnecessary adjectives and adverbs; muddled tenses; a lack of helpful sequence words.) Add notes to the edges of the text and save the work for tomorrow's lesson.	

DAY 2 ■ Agreeing on diagrams

Key features	Stages	Additional opportunities
	### Introduction Return to yesterday's text and notes. Discuss the notes with the children. Experiment with the text as you agree on the changes that need to be made. Emphasise the need for your instructions to be as clear as possible as you demonstrate editing. Suggest that you do not want to add any more words to the instructions. Ask the children: *What else will convey information?* (Diagrams.)	**Phonics:** *each*, bl*ow* **HFW:** ball, then
Communication: work collaboratively in group contexts	### Independent work Suggest that the children agree on three diagrams to accompany the instructions. They can work in groups of three, each drawing one diagram. They also need to decide where the diagrams would be best placed.	
Social skills: listen to and respect other people's contributions	### Plenary Bring the groups together into discussion groups of six. The new group must share ideas and agree on the best one or two diagrams to add.	

DAY 3 ■ Organising the layout

Key features	Stages	Additional opportunities
	Introduction Display your PE instructions. Remind the children that you decided to add diagrams. Emphasise that the diagrams must clarify the text. Return to yesterday's groups of six. Listen to each group's two diagram proposals before you agree on your final choices as a class. Add the diagrams to your modelled writing. Remind the children about electronic instructions (see Phase 1, Day 3). Ask: *How would an electronic text link to a diagram?* (Using a hyperlink.)	**Phonics:** *each*, bl*ow* **HFW:** ball, then
Communication: work collaboratively in paired and group contexts	**Speaking and listening** Invite the children to discuss with their partners if and where they would use hyperlinks if they were putting these instruction on a website.	
	Independent work Let partners discuss the new version of the instructions. Could they improve the layout? Encourage them to consider organisational devices (such as bullet points), as well as hyperlinks if you are using an interactive whiteboard. Ask the children to plan individually the clearest look for your instructions.	**Support:** use partner work
Social skills: listen to and respect other people's contributions	**Plenary** Share ideas, discussing and finalising choices. If you can, include hyperlinks in your instructions.	

Guided writing

Read photocopiable page 105 'How to act in our classroom' together. Model how to write instructions for a different part of the school day. For example: preparing for a PE lesson or queuing for lunch. Children can add their own diagrams.

Assessment

First, write a simple sentence beginning with an imperative. Then write the sentence an alternative way, beginning with a connective indicating the sequence of events (*First, Next, Then*).

Question the children:

Which is a good connective to start with?

Which could follow on?

Refer back to the learning outcomes on page 91.

Further work

Ask the children to add new instructions to photocopiable page 105 'How to act in our classroom'. Remind them about hyperlinks. Provide access to the computer so that they can include a hyperlink (perhaps to a diagram of a happy face, or of a wastepaper bin) in their additions.

DAY 1 ▪ Writing instructions

Key features	Stages	Additional opportunities
Enquiry: ask questions arising from work in another area of the curriculum	**Introduction** Remind the children about the instructions for making a folding book you wrote together (Sequence 1, Phase 3). Display the modelled instructions and class instruction checklist (Phase 3, Day 4). Demonstrate how to check the modelled instructions against the checklist. Explain that you want the children to use the checklist to guide them in writing new instructions for playing a game (perhaps a playtime or PE game with a limited choice of equipment). Children could also use the Instruction skeleton from the CD-ROM to help structure their writing.	**Phonics:** *game* **HFW:** what, you
Communication: work collaboratively in paired and whole-class contexts	**Speaking and listening** Suggest that the children share ideas with their partners before you talk about possibilities as a class. **Independent work** Ask the children to begin by deciding what game their instructions are for. The title must make this clear. As they make notes, they should progress to the *What you need* section.	
Evaluation: give instructions orally and in writing	**Plenary** Discuss with the class the need for trial and error. For example: identifying that a title could be improved or that something is missing from their *What you need* section. Encourage the children to think of their early work as a first draft so they will feel comfortable about making alterations.	

DAY 2 ▪ Using the instruction

Key features	Stages	Additional opportunities
	Introduction Remind the children about the instructions they are writing. Suggest that the instructions will be for a child of their own age, perhaps in a different class. Display the class checklist (Phase 3, Day 4), and remind the children of how you checked the modelled writing against it.	**Phonics:** *game* **HFW:** what, you
	Speaking and listening Let the children compare titles with their partners. Does the title make it clear what the instructions will be about? Do they need to make changes?	
Reasoning: sequence actions logically to form a set of instructions	**Independent work** Give each child a copy of the checklist. Encourage them to refer to this as they write their game instructions. Suggest that they say their instructions to themselves, testing that they work, as they write.	**Support:** work with children and help them to evaluate their work
Evaluation: give instructions orally and in writing	**Plenary** Listen to sample pairs of lines. Is their consistent use of tenses? Should some words be left out? Does the sequence seem correct?	

DAY 3 ■ Using sequence words

Key features	Stages	Additional opportunities
	Introduction Remind the children how using sequence words can improve instructions. Highlight examples in the modelled instructions (Sequence 1, Phase 3). Display the checklist (Phase 3, Day 4) and return to yesterday's work.	**Phonics:** check, game **HFW:** what, make, then
	Speaking and listening Encourage the children to discuss with their partners what sort of diagrams would make their instructions clearer.	
Reasoning: sequence actions logically to form a set of instructions	**Independent work** Let the children finalise their writing. Remind them to keep using the checklist. Ask them to add at least one detailed diagram to their instructions.	
Evaluation: give instructions orally and in writing	**Plenary** Create a display of sequence words as the children tell you ones they have used. What other devices have they used to indicate sequence?	

DAY 4 ■ Evaluating the instructions

Key features	Stages	Additional opportunities
	Introduction Return to the children's finished writing from yesterday.	**Phonics:** check, test, game **HFW:** what, make, then
	Speaking and listening Use partner and then class discussion to consider the best ways to evaluate these written instructions. Agree on the need for testing.	
Communication: work collaboratively in paired and whole-class contexts	**Independent work** Provide equipment and ask partners to exchange, follow and evaluate each other's written instructions. Allow time for written and oral exchange of conclusions. Let everyone use these conclusions for a final self-appraisal. What will they need to do to make their instructions even clearer next time?	**Extend:** children can put the instructions together to create a class book of new games for PE
Evaluation: judge the effectiveness of their own work	**Plenary** Discuss the evaluation results. What was the main fault? How do children plan to improve? Make a list of important points and save a copy.	

Guided reading

Work with the children as they read one another's instructions in small groups. Ask them to identify features common to all the instructions. Which feature do they find particularly important? Why?

Assessment

Use the 'Writing instructions' photocopiable assessment activity from the CD-ROM for the children to write instructions for a new game. Refer back to the learning outcomes on page 91.

Further work

After reading a partner's instructions, ask the children to mark them against the checklist. Let partners give feedback to each other. Finally, the children can write a self-evaluation of their success.

How to make a Chinese New Year lantern

Next fold it in half, lengthways.

First take a piece of red paper.

Finally join the edges with sticky tape.

After that cut about six slits from the fold, half way to the edge.

Then roll it up loosely from the bottom to the top.

When you have made the cuts, open the paper out fully.

What you need: ■ red paper   ■ scissors   ■ sticky tape

How to act in our classroom

A How to come in	B How to pack up
Come in quietly.	Put your books in your drawer.
Have a smile on your face.	Pick up bits from under your place.
Put your things away.	Put the bits in the bin.
Go to your place.	Check that you have your homework.
Then sit down.	Tuck your chair under the table.
C How to answer the register	**D How to ask a question**
Listen for your name.	Put your hand up.
Answer when you hear your name.	Go to the teacher if you need to.
Say "Good morning" or "Good afternoon". Speak clearly.	Wait until the teacher sees you.
Sound cheerful.	Then ask your question.
	Listen to the answer.

Checklist for instructions

☐ A title that says what the instructions are for

_____

☐ At the beginning, a list of what is needed

_____

☐ Instructions in the correct order

_____

☐ Words or symbols that make the order clear

_____

☐ Some time and sequence words

_____

☐ Verbs in the right tense

_____

☐ Diagrams

_____

☐ A helpful layout

_____

   PHOTOCOPIABLE ■**SCHOLASTIC** www.scholastic.co.uk

NON-FICTION
UNIT 2 Explanations

Speak and listen for a range of purposes on paper and on screen

Strand 1 Speaking
- Explain ideas and processes using imaginative and adventurous vocabulary and non-verbal gestures to support communication.

Strand 2 Listening and responding
- Listen to others in class, ask relevant questions and follow instructions.
- Listen to talk by an adult, remember some specific points and identify what they have learned.

Strand 3 Group discussion and interaction
- Ensure that everyone contributes, allocate tasks, and consider alternatives and reach agreement.

Read for a range of purposes on paper and on screen

Strand 5 Word recognition: decoding (reading) and encoding (spelling)
- Read independently and with increasing fluency longer and less familiar texts.
- Read high and medium frequency words independently and automatically.

Strand 6 Word structure and spelling
- Spell with increasing accuracy and confidence, drawing on word recognition and knowledge of word structure and spelling patterns including common inflections and use of double letters.
- Read and spell less common alternative graphemes including trigraphs.

Strand 7 Understanding and interpreting texts
- Give some reasons why things happen or characters change.
- Explain organisational features of texts, including alphabetical order, layout, diagrams, captions, hyperlinks and bullet points.

Strand 8 Engaging with and responding to texts
- Engage with books through exploring and enacting interpretations.

Write for a range of purposes on paper and on screen

Strand 9 Creating and shaping texts
- Draw on knowledge and experience of texts in deciding and planning what and how to write.
- Select from different presentational features to suit particular writing purposes on paper and on screen.

Strand 10 Text structure and organisation
- Use planning to establish clear sections for writing.
- Use appropriate language to make sections hang together.

Strand 11 Sentence structure and punctuation
- Write simple and compound sentences and begin to use subordination in relation to time and reason.

Progression in explanatory texts

In this year, children are moving towards:
- Creating a flowchart or cyclical diagram to explain a process, as a member of a group with the teacher.
- After seeing and hearing an oral explanation of a process, explaining the same process orally also using flowchart, language and gestures appropriately.

UNIT 2 ◄ Explanations continued

- Reading, with help, flowcharts or cyclical diagrams explaining other processes and then read others independently.
- Producing a simple flowchart or cyclical diagram independently.

Key aspects of learning covered in this Unit

Enquiry
Children will carry out their own enquiry or investigation in another area of the curriculum, and will make observations and explain what they have found out. Children will be encouraged to pose questions prior to, during and after their investigation and decide the most appropriate presentation for their findings.

Information processing
Children will identify relevant information from observation and practical experience, information texts and ICT texts and select this to help them write their own explanation text for an individual or class book or wall display.

Evaluation
Children will present information orally and in writing, in the form of a flowchart or cyclical diagram. They will be able to support their judgements with their own evidence, drawing on a range of sources to support their evaluation.

Communication
Children will develop their ability to express and communicate in spoken, pictorial and written form a simple explanation of a process. They may also communicate their ideas using a variety of prompts.

Prior learning

Before starting this Unit check that the children can:
- Use alphabetical order to access simple dictionaries and glossaries.
- Read simple definitions and explanations.
- Write simple reports – explanations require many of the same language structures as reports, but explanations are an extension of report texts in that they explain phenomena, rather than simply describe them.
- Contribute to class discussions on the use of conjunctions which relate to cause and effect, for example *because* and *so*.

If they need further support please refer to a prior Unit or a similar Unit in Year 1.

Resources

Phase 1:
Index by Eileen Jones ❀; *How does a battery make a bulb light up?* (text and flowchart versions) by Eileen Jones ❀; Interactive activity 'Alphabetical order' ❀

Phase 2:
How does a battery make a bulb light up? (text version) by Eileen Jones ❀; Photocopiable page 119 'Features of an explanation text'; Photocopiable page 120 'Construct'; Interactive activity 'Construct' ❀

Phase 3:
How does an acorn become a tree? (text version) by Eileen Jones ❀; Photocopiable page 121 'Explanation text'

Phase 4:
Photocopiable page 122 'Review form'; *How does an acorn become a tree?* (flowchart version) ❀; Assessment activity 'Growing up' ❀

Cross-curricular opportunities

Science – Using electricity; Plants and animals in the local environment

UNIT 2 ■ Teaching sequence

Phase	Children's objectives	Summary of activities	Learning outcomes
1	I can identify key words. I can use an index to find information in a book. I can put words in alphabetical order. I can make a glossary. I understand how diagrams are used in non-fiction texts.	List key words related to electricity investigation. Identify how to find information through key words. Use alphabetical order for an index. Write glossary definitions. Suggest diagrams to add to explanation text.	Children can find a key word using an index and then locate the relevant information on a page. Children can demonstrate that they have understood information read from a book or screen by noting the main points. Children can make and use a class glossary of special interest words related to the investigation and give explanations and definitions. Children can follow a line of enquiry emerging from their own questions.
2	I can identify key features of explanation texts. I can construct sentences with conjunctions. I can identify three ways of presenting an explanation. I can make a group flowchart.	Identify key features of explanation texts. Construct sentences with conjunctions. Make a group human flowchart.	Children can use technical vocabulary and causal connectives to explain a phenomenon. Children can model a process using models, pictures and diagrams and explain the process to peers.
3	I can make an explanation text clearer by adding diagrams. I can make a pictorial flowchart.	Plan diagrams to clarify text. Construct a pictorial flowchart.	Children can recognise structure and language features of explanation text. Children can make choices about the best way to present information in an explanation text, using flowcharts and diagrams.
4	I can recognise a cyclical flowchart. I can write an explanation text. I can present and evaluate explanations.	Discuss a cyclical diagram; collaborate on writing an explanation text on screen. Write independently. Add a diagram. Present and evaluate.	Children can note information collected from more than one source, including their own practical work in another curriculum area. Children can visual representation that models a process. Children can write and evaluate explanation texts.

Provide copies of the objectives for the children.

DAY 1 ■ Key words

Key features	Stages	Additional opportunities
Information processing: identify relevant information for a practical experience	**Introduction** Using what they have learned in a different curriculum area remind the children about an investigation they have done. For example making a circuit during the electricity topic in science. Mention one word that is important to the work and write it on the board. **Speaking and listening** Let partners question each other about the investigation process. For example: *What was the aim of the investigation? What steps did we carry out?* **Independent work** Suggest that the children are preparing a list for another child to do this same investigation next year. Ask them, independently or with their partner, to list about ten key words related to the work. Encourage them to work from memory before referring back to their science book. **Plenary** Share results as a class. Agree on 12 to 15 of the most important words and add them to the whiteboard, writing them down in random order. Save these words.	**Phonics:** *make*, *bulb* **HFW:** do, ten **Support:** children can write five words **Extend:** children can write more words

DAY 2 ■ Using an index

Key features	Stages	Additional opportunities
Information processing: identify relevant information for a practical experience	**Introduction** Choose a topic that the children have already covered in a different curriculum area this year, such as the Great Fire of London. Select a history resource book with information on the Great Fire and an index; a glossary would also be useful. Do not show the children the book. Remind the children of this history work. Explain that at the beginning of the year you chose a book to use. **Speaking and listening** Ask the children: *How could I tell (without reading the whole book) it had the Great Fire in it?* Encourage them to discuss the answers with their partners. Share ideas as a class. Agree on a title page's preliminary importance. Reveal your book, analysing the information on its title page: title, series name, illustration. Ask: *Is this book likely to be factual or fictional?* **Independent work** Put the children into groups of four. Let them remind one another of facts, or questions about the Great Fire (For example: *Where did it start?*) They must decide, in small discussion groups, how to find out (without reading the whole book) if their information is mentioned in your book. **Plenary** Share ideas. Are key words important? What about an index? Demonstrate how to use your book's index to find references to Pudding Lane.	**Phonics:** *lane*, *start* **HFW:** help, could

DAY 3 ■ Alphabetical order

Key features	Stages	Additional opportunities
	Introduction Remind the children of your book from yesterday. Ask them: *Which part of the book did we find very useful? Why?* Open *Index* from the CD-ROM. Explain that this is part of the index from a history book. Ask: *What do you notice? Are the words in any order?*	**Phonics:** l*a*ne, st*a*rt, *or*der **HFW:** help, could
Information processing: identify relevant information from an information text	**Speaking and listening** Encourage the children to discuss with their partners if and why alphabetical order helps them if they want to find out if *Pudding Lane* is referred to in the book. Share class views. Agree that alphabetical order makes checking quicker. Display and remind the children of the electricity words from Day 1.	
	Independent work Ask the children, in pairs, to choose three of the words they may have used in their electricity investigation. They can list them (like an index) in alphabetical order, on their individual whiteboards.	**Support:** give children an alphabet line **Extend:** children progress to the interactive activity on the CD-ROM
Evaluation: present information in writing	**Plenary** Let the children hold up their boards for others to check. Are all the words in correct alphabetical order? Should any change places? Create a list on the whiteboard of all the words and work together to put them into alphabetical order. Save the list.	

DAY 4 ■ Creating a glossary

Key features	Stages	Additional opportunities
	Introduction Display yesterday's alphabetical list of electricity words. Highlight an important one, for example *connection*. Ask: *What does it mean?* Agree on a short definition, for example *link*, and write it next to the word.	**Phonics:** m*ea*n, w*or*d **HFW:** next, three, two
	Speaking and listening Let the children work with yesterday's partners to compose definitions for their three words.	
Evaluation: present information in writing	**Independent work** Suggest that everyone works out definitions for two words and writes them on their individual whiteboards. Play a game where a selected child reads out a definition. Whoever guesses the word has the next turn. The agreed definition is written next to the word.	**Support:** children work in pairs **Extend:** children prepare more than two definitions
	Plenary Discuss the completed list. Do the children know what they have made? Have they ever noticed a *glossary* at the back of a factual book? Show them an example in a book you have in the classroom. Examine some of the book's text. Are words highlighted to indicate their inclusion in the glossary?	

DAY 5 ▮ Introducing flowcharts

Key features	Stages	Additional opportunities

Introduction
Display and read aloud *How does a battery make a bulb light up?* (text version) from the CD-ROM. Ask the children: *What does the text explain? Why are some words highlighted?* (They are defined in the glossary.)
Underline *because, so* and *but*.

Phonics: store, wire
HFW: because, two

Speaking and listening
Allow the children to discuss with their partners the role of the underlined words. What type of words are they? (Conjunctions.)
Come together as a class. Analyse the effect of these conjunctions. Agree that they explain either cause or effect.

Communication:
communicate their ideas using diagrams and charts

Independent work
Working with a partner, ask the children to plan a diagram that explains the process outlined in the text. Will they use labels and captions?
Set a time limit so that children will have time to present their work.

Plenary
Share the results and encourage partners to use words and gestures to explain their diagrams. Has anyone thought of using a flowchart? Explain what this is, and display and discuss the *How does a battery make a bulb light up?* (flowchart version) from the CD-ROM. Ask the children: *How does the flowchart work? Why are arrows helpful to the reader?*

Guided reading
Give out copies of the text from Day 5. Suggest that children read it in a group with your teaching assistant.
Ask the children: *Which words would you put in a glossary? What would be the correct order for the words? What definitions would you provide?*

Assessment
Relate the task to science work you have covered, by asking the children to read a short text in one of your classroom books.
Use questioning to assess if the children can:
■ understand the content of the text;
■ answer a question related to the text;
■ identify a key word;
■ use the book's index;
■ find an appropriate page for a question's answer.
Refer back to the learning outcomes on page 109.

Further work
Refer to a recent design and technology project completed by the children. Suggest they need to identify the key words relating to this project. Ask them to create a personal glossary containing these key words.

DAY 1 ■ Features of an explanation text

Key features	Stages	Additional opportunities
	Introduction Re-read *How does a battery make a bulb light up?* (text version) from the CD-ROM with the children. Ask: *What text type is it? Why are words highlighted?* Underline *because, so* and *but*.	**Phonics:** sto*re*, *wi*re **HFW:** because, so, but
Communication: develop their ability to express in written form a simple explanation of a process	**Speaking and listening** Ask the children to tell their partners what class of words the underlined words belong to. What is their job? What do these three words help to tell the reader? Come together as a class. Explain that these are cause and effect conjunctions – a usual feature of explanations. Continue to move between partner and class oral work, using questions to draw out other key features of written explanations. Ask: *What word begins the title? What is special about the title?* (It's a question.) *What type of sentence starts the explanation? What is its purpose?* (It's a general statement of introduction.) *Is the information in a particular order? What else would be helpful?* (A diagram.)	
	Independent work Give the children photocopiable page 119 'Features of an explanation text'. Ask them, individually or with partners, to test their memories by filling in the missing words.	**Support:** children work with partners or with adult support **Extend:** children identify where each feature appears in the electricity text
	Plenary Compare the children's answers. Compile and display an explanation checklist.	

DAY 2 ■ Constructing sentences

Key features	Stages	Additional opportunities
	Introduction Talk about the need for explanations to make sense. Challenge the children to a game in which they must choose the words to finish your sentence. Play the interactive 'Construct' game from the CD-ROM. For each sentence, allow thinking time before individuals or partners write their chosen letter. As children hold up their individual whiteboards, agree on the majority decision and try it out. Is the class right? Discuss how the children reached their decisions. Were facts or language used? Did conjunctions ending the first half of the sentences affect the second half?	**Phonics:** pl*a*nt, r*ai*n **HFW:** because, so
Communication: develop their ability to express in written form a simple explanation of a process	**Independent work** Make copies of photocopiable page 120 'Construct' and cut them up. Give the children a strip of card with half a sentence on it. They must find someone with a strip that completes their sentence. Let each child find a partner. If they can construct a sentence, they go and sit in your 'Construct' circle on the carpet.	**Support:** children work with a partner **Extend:** children work with partners to write and construct a new sentence using a time conjunction
	Plenary Ask pairs of children to stand together and say their connected sentence. Does it sound right? Use discussion to emphasise why some make more sense than others. Experiment with changing connectives. Stress the effect of different connectives. Play this or the interactive game again.	

DAY 3 ■ Sunflower flowcharts

Key features	Stages	Additional opportunities

Stages

Introduction

Display *How does a battery make a bulb light up?* (text and flowchart versions) from the CD-ROM to remind the children of the two ways in which an electricity circuit was explained. Ask: *What third method of presentation did you think of?* (A diagram.)

Speaking and listening

Ask the children to discuss with their partners or in small groups which methods of presentation they prefer. Hold a class vote on which method is clearest.

Progress to a new curriculum area, reminding the children of a familiar process for example, the development of a seed into a sunflower.

Independent work

Put the children into discussion groups of four to six to plan a flowchart, with each group member drawing a picture to represent a stage in the sunflower process.

Let groups rehearse arranging themselves into a human flowchart, holding their pictures and saying appropriate words of explanation as their step of the process is reached.

Plenary

Watch and listen to the group flowcharts. Do the audience find the explanations clear?

Key features

Information processing: identify relevant information from practical experience
Evaluation: present information in the form of a flowchart

Additional opportunities

Phonics: chart, seed
HFW: how, yellow

Guided reading

Provide the children with two explanatory texts from classroom resource books on a relevant topic, such as electricity.
Ask the children to discuss the texts in a group with your teaching assistant.
They should compare the explanations and the range of presentation methods.

Assessment

Using information from the text used in the guided reading activity, ask the children to speak for one minute about electricity for example: they could speak about a classroom appliance that uses electricity and explain the associated dangers.
Assess if the children are able to give an oral explanation.
Refer back to the learning outcomes on page 109.

Further work

Suggest that the children add to their assessment explanations. (For example: why the appliance functions when it is plugged into the electrical socket.)
Encourage the use of causal and time connectives.

DAY 1 ■ Reaching a conclusion

Key features	Stages	Additional opportunities
	Introduction Display and read aloud *How does an acorn become a tree?* from the CD-ROM. Ask the children: *What text type is it? What important features do you recognise? What connectives are used?* Identify time as well as causal ones. Highlight the final paragraph.	**Phonics:** in*si*de, gr*ou*nd **HFW:** an, by, so
Communication: develop their ability to express and communicate in pictorial and written form a simple explanation of a process	**Speaking and listening** Ask the children to discuss with their partners: *What job does the final paragraph have?* Share ideas as a class. Agree that in the final paragraph the explanation reaches a conclusion and completes the explanation in answer to the *How...?* title. Point out these points on the photocopiable page 119 'Features of an explanation text'.	
	Independent work Let small groups plan the diagrams they would add to this text. What would they include? What about captions, labels or charts? Where would they place them?	**Support:** ask your teaching assistant to suggest diagrams that the children could add
	Plenary Listen and watch the children's presentations as they justify their methods of making this text clearer. Do other children think the text would be improved? Who makes the strongest case?	

DAY 2 ■ A pictorial flowchart

Key features	Stages	Additional opportunities
	Introduction Remind the children of a recent science or design and technology investigation where they have had practical experience. What was the process involved?	**Phonics:** ch*a*rt, gr*ou*p **HFW:** next, then
Enquiry: decide the most appropriate presentation for their findings	**Speaking and listening** Ask the children to share their ideas with their partner and then with the rest of the class about how they could they could explain the process to someone else.	
Communication: communicate ideas using diagrams and charts **Evaluation:** present information in the format of a flowchart	**Independent work** Put the children into groups of four to six. Invite them to create pictures and model a human flowchart of the process, with each member (or pair) in the group representing a stage of the process. Reduce groups to pairs for the children to each construct their own flowchart in pictorial form. Use photocopiable page 121 'Explanation text'.	**Extend:** children can import their diagrams into presentational software and create a slideshow
	Plenary If possible, scan the children's pictorial flowcharts into the computer so that they can present them on the interactive whiteboard. Encourage them to use language and gestures to explain their work. Ask the children to save their flowcharts.	

Guided reading

Suggest the children work together with your teaching assistant to read the text *How does an acorn become a tree?* from the CD-ROM. Ask them to Identify conjunctions.

Can they find an effective place to add a time conjunction?

What would the time conjunction be?

Assessment

Set the task of thinking about the process of an acorn becoming a tree. Ask them to talk about the pictures they would use to make the explanation clear.

Can they explain orally how the pictures would create a pictorial flowchart?

Refer back to the learning outcomes on page 109.

Further work

Return to the assessment task. Let the children present their pictorial flowcharts as a poster.

DAY 1 ■ Cyclical flowcharts

Key features	Stages	Additional opportunities
	### Introduction Display the *How does an acorn become a tree?* cyclical flowchart from the CD-ROM. Talk it through with the children.	**Phonics:** ins*ide*, gr*ou*nd **HFW:** an, by, so, because
	### Speaking and listening Ask the children to talk to a partner about the pictures. What has happened to the acorn? What will grow on the tree? (Acorns.) Suggest that the process follows a cycle. Demonstrate how to write an explanation text based on the flowchart. Use an opening statement and then begin a series of logical steps. Emphasise constructing sentences and using connectives of reason and cause.	
Communication: communicate in written form a simple explanation of a process	### Independent work Pause to let the children plan the next step of writing with their talking partners. Listen to suggested sentences, encouraging changes so that the children use *because* and *so*. Then write up the next part. Continue with the children planning with a talking partner and then you writing up each step. Leave the children to write the final section(s), using paired reading and re-reading of their writing to check for cohesion and use of the present tense.	
	### Plenary Listen to the children's text and finalise your writing. Emphasise the need for a conclusion. Check the writing against your explanation checklist (see Phase 2, Day 1).	

DAY 2 ■ Writing an explanation text

Key features	Stages	Additional opportunities
Information processing: select information to write their explanation text	### Introduction Return to the pictorial flowcharts from Phase 3, Day 2. Explain to the children that you are making a display explaining the process shown in these charts. Do oral revision of the investigation, collaborating to create a glossary of key words. Ask: *What order are the words in?* Together, write brief definitions. The children must write an explanation text for the display, using their pictorial flowchart as their plan. The display will be looked at by children who have not done the investigation themselves so explanations need to be clear. Write a *How* or *Why* title on the whiteboard.	**Phonics:** *how, order* **HFW:** how, because, so
Communication: communicate in written form a simple explanation of a process	### Independent work Let the children read and makes notes on their pictorial plan of any additional information needed. Encourage them to use different sources, perhaps a text book, their exercise book and discussion with other children. They can then start writing their text and refer to the checklist as they work. Encourage oral rehearsal (to themselves or a response partner) as the children write, edit and make changes. ### Plenary Discuss the children's progress.	**Support:** children rehearse oral sentences and then write text for each picture **Extend:** children progress to drawing an accompanying diagram

DAY 3 ■ Finalising the explanation texts

Key features	Stages	Additional opportunities
	Introduction Remind the children of the texts they began yesterday.	**Phonics:** *how, mark* **HFW:** *how, because, so*
Evaluation: present information in writing **Enquiry:** decide the most appropriate presentation for their findings	**Independent work** Ask the children to complete their writing, making sure they have covered all the points on the checklist. They must decide whether or not to add a picture or diagram. Encourage them to make a final review and check of their own work, before they ask a writing partner to review it and suggest necessary editing. Suggest that the children think how they will present their explanation. Ask: *What written text will be read? What diagram or picture will be looked at and read? What oral words, spoken by you, will be heard?* Give each child a copy of photocopiable page 122 'Review form' and put the children into pairs. As a child makes their presentation to a partner, the partner can record an assessment of how well the written, visual and verbal information is given.	**Support:** children use ticks and crosses to mark clarity of partner's explanation
	Plenary Come together as a class. Ask: *What have you learned about explanations? Do most people prefer text or diagrams? Is a mixture of both clearest?*	**Extend:** children provide oral and written feedback

Guided reading
Work with groups of children to read and compare two explanation texts linked to relevant curriculum work.
What important explanation features can they identify?

Assessment
Ask children to complete the interactive assessment activity 'Growing up' on the CD-ROM. Refer back to the learning outcomes on page 109.

Further work
Look at the CD-ROM interactive assessment. Ask the children to produce a pictorial flowchart for this sequence.

Features of an explanation text

diagram	conjunctions	how	reader
present	sentence	happen	
conclusion	why	question	

The heading is often a_____ .

The heading often begins_____ or_____ .

Verbs are in the_____ tense.

The introduction is a statement _____ .

Cause and effect_____ are used.

Information is written in the order things_____ .

A_____ is helpful to the_____ .

There must be a_____ .

Construct

Set 1

The plant grows faster in the garden because

The plant grows faster in the garden so

The plant grows faster in the garden but

The plant grows faster in the garden and

Set 2

it reaches my height more quickly.

it has plenty of food and sun.

it would grow even faster with more rain.

it flowers faster too.

Explanation text

How _____ ?

Review form

■ How clear is the explanation?

■ Write your comments in the boxes.

	Written text	Diagram	Spoken words
What I found clear:			
What I did not find clear:			
Improvements I would make:			

NON-FICTION
UNIT 3 Information texts

Speak and listen for a range of purposes on paper and on screen

Strand 1 Speaking
■ Explain ideas and processes using imaginative and adventurous vocabulary and non-verbal gestures to support communication.

Strand 2 Listening and responding
■ Listen to others in class, ask relevant questions and follow instructions.

Strand 3 Group discussion and interaction
■ Listen to each other's views and preferences, agree the next steps to take and identify contributions by each group member.

Read for a range of purposes on paper and on screen

Strand 5 Word recognition: decoding (reading) and encoding (spelling)
■ Read independently and with increasing fluency longer and less familiar texts.
■ Read high and medium frequency words independently and automatically.

Strand 6 Word structure and spelling
■ Spell with increasing accuracy and confidence, drawing on word recognition and knowledge of word structure and spelling patterns.
■ Read and spell less common alternative graphemes including trigraphs.

Strand 7 Understanding and interpreting texts
■ Draw together ideas and information from across a whole text, using signposts in the text.
■ Explain organisational features of texts.
■ Explain how particular words are used, including words and expressions with similar meanings.

Strand 8 Engaging with and responding to texts
■ Explain their reactions to texts, commenting on important aspects.

Write for a range of purposes on paper and on screen

Strand 9 Creating and shaping texts
■ Draw on knowledge and experience of texts in deciding and planning what and how to write.
■ Make adventurous word and language choices.
■ Select from different presentational features to suit writing purposes.

Strand 10 Text structure and organisation
■ Use planning to establish clear sections for writing.
■ Use appropriate language to make sections hang together.

Strand 11 Sentence structure and punctuation
■ Write simple and compound sentences and begin to use subordination in relation to time and reason.
■ Compose sentences using tense consistently (present and past).
■ Use question marks and use commas to separate items in a list.

Strand 12 Presentation
■ Word-process short narrative and non-narrative texts.

Progression in information texts

In this year, children are moving towards:
■ Using contents pages and alphabetically ordered texts.

UNIT 3 ◄ Information texts *continued*

- Scanning texts to find specific sections and skim-reading to speculate what a book might be about and evaluate its usefulness for the research in hand.
- Scanning a website to find specific sections.
- Making simple notes from non-fiction texts to use in subsequent writing.
- Writing simple information texts.
- Designing and creating a simple ICT text.

Key aspects of learning covered in this Unit

Enquiry
Children will ask questions arising from work in another area of the curriculum, research and then plan how to present the information effectively.

Information processing
Children will identify relevant information from a range of sources on paper and on screen and use this to write their own information texts.

Evaluation
Children will present information orally and in writing. They will discuss success criteria, give feedback to others and judge the effectiveness of their own work.

Communication
Children will develop their ability to discuss as they work collaboratively in paired, group and whole-class contexts. They will develop their ability to listen critically to broadcast information and to make an oral presentation. They will also communicate outcomes in writing.

Prior learning

Before starting this Unit check that the children can:
- Scan texts for information.
- Offer opinions about the suitability of a text for research.

If they need further support please refer to a prior Unit or a similar Unit in Year 1.

Resources

Sequence 1, Phase 1:
Interactive activity 'What's in the book?' ✵

Sequence 1, Phase 2:
The Great Fire of London by Eileen Jones ✵; *The Great Fire of London* (differentiated version) by Eileen Jones ✵; Photocopiable page 138 'Florence Nightingale'; Photograph of Florence Nightingale ✵; Recording of Florence Nightingale's voice ✵

Sequence 1, Phase 3:
Florence Nightingale by Eileen Jones ✵; *Florence Nightingale* (differentiated version) by Eileen Jones ✵; Photocopiable page 139 'Useful sources'

Sequence 2, Phase 1:
Common wild flowers by David Waugh ✵; Interactive activity 'What's in the book?'

Sequence 2, Phase 2:
Common wild flowers by David Waugh ✵

Sequence 2, Phase 3:
Photocopiable page 140 'Evaluation'; Interactive activity 'What's in the book?' ✵; Assessment activity 'Plants glossary' ✵

Cross-curricular opportunities

Science – Plants and animals in the local environment
History – The Great Fire of London; Famous people
ICT – Communicating information using text; Finding information

UNIT 3 ■ Teaching sequence 1

Phase	Children's objectives	Summary of activities	Learning outcomes
1	I can ask questions. I know where to start looking for information in a book. I can use a dictionary.	Pose and record questions for investigation. Compile a contents page. Use dictionaries and alphabetical order.	Children can pose questions for investigation and understand the layout of information in a factual book..
2	I can find information on a website. I can make notes from an ICT text. I can discuss a recording and ask questions.	Collaborate in investigating a website. Find information on a website independently. Discuss a recording and pose and record questions for investigation	Children can make simple notes from books and ICT texts.
3	I can make notes from an ICT text. I can make notes from a variety of different non-fiction books. I can compare ICT texts and books and evaluate their usefulness.	Make independent notes from ICT text Make independent notes from books Evaluate research material	Children can do research and make simple notes from books and ICT texts.

UNIT 3 ■ Teaching sequence 2

Phase	Children's objectives	Summary of activities	Learning outcomes
1	I can plan an information book and write a contents page. I can write chapters of a book using my notes.	Write a contents page. Write chapters and plan illustrations for a non-fiction book.	Children can convert notes into a non-narrative text.
2	I can design a simple website. I can create a simple website.	Complete chapters. Investigate website features. Design a simple website. Create a website.	Children can design and create a simple website.
3	I can write a glossary. I write an index. I can make a cover for my book and evaluate it. I can give feedback on other children's books.	Add a glossary. Add an index. Add cover and evaluate own work. Read and evaluate other children's texts.	Children complete and evaluate a simple information text.

Provide copies of the objectives for the children.

DAY 1 ◼ Asking questions

Key features	Stages	Additional opportunities
	### Introduction Present the children with a scenario: they, as children who have just moved to your class from Year 1, have been told that they are going to learn about the Great Fire of London.	**Phonics:** f*i*re, wh*e*re **HFW:** when, who, where, what
Enquiry: ask questions arising from work in another area of the curriculum	### Speaking and listening Ask the children to exchange ideas with their partner on the first question they would ask about the Great Fire. Listen to the children's suggestions and write one on the whiteboard. For example: *When was the Great Fire?*	
Communication: work collaboratively in paired and whole-class contexts	### Independent work Let the children continue their partner discussions as they think of another four likely questions. They will need to write them down and save them for the next Phase.	
	### Plenary Listen to the children's results and write and display many on the whiteboard. Add one or two of your own, deliberately choosing questions that the children still cannot answer. Save these questions.	

DAY 2 ◼ Contents

Key features	Stages	Additional opportunities
	### Introduction Hold up a factual book on plants and pose a question about plants.	**Phonics:** f*i*re, wh*e*re **HFW:** when, who, where, what
Information processing: identify information from a range of sources	### Speaking and listening Ask the children to discuss with their partners: *How can I find out where to find the answer without reading the whole book?* Come together as a class and share the children's ideas. Use the term 'contents' and show them the contents page of your book. Comment on its position in the book. What is its purpose? What about the numbers at the side? Read out the section or chapter headings. Ask: *Which sounds useful to me?* Display yesterday's questions about The Great Fire of London and open the 'What's in the book?' interactive activity from the CD-ROM. Suggest that the author of this book, on the Great Fire has not finished the chapter headings. Display yesterday's questions. Suggest you hope the planned chapters will be appropriate for the class's questions.	
Communication: work collaboratively in paired and whole-class contexts	### Independent work Print copies of the 'What's in the book?' page from the CD-ROM. In pairs, or individually, let the children complete the contents with chapter titles to suit their questions.	
	### Plenary Compare and discuss headings and wording. Collaborate on a final version, using an interactive whiteboard if possible. Keep a copy of the contents.	

DAY 3 ■ Making an illustrated dictionary

Key features	Stages	Additional opportunities
	Introduction Display 'What's in the book?' from the CD-ROM or your completed version. Point out *Index* and *Glossary*. What do the terms mean? Which tells you where to find information? Which words are in the glossary?	**Phonics:** *powder* **HFW:** *where*
	Speaking and listening Encourage the children to discuss with their partners other ways that we can find word meanings. Share ideas as a class, comparing a dictionary's greater number of words with the certainty of a highlighted word's inclusion in a glossary.	
Information processing: identify relevant information and use this to write their own information texts	**Independent work** Put the children into pairs giving them six small squares of paper. Write on the whiteboard: *pail, cathedral, thatch, gunpowder, diary.* Encourage partners to take turns finding a word in the dictionary and reading out its definition. Can they make the meaning clearer in their own words? They must write the words with brief meanings and draw illustrations on the pieces of paper before laying them out in alphabetical order. Can they create another page for their illustrated dictionary, with a history or science word beginning with a different letter?	**Extend:** give children additional words **Support:** give children three words
Evaluation: present information in writing	**Plenary** Compare the children's results. Are everyone's dictionary pages in the same order? Are the pictures useful?	

Guided reading

Ask groups of children to read a contents page from a classroom information book. Come together as a class and ask a volunteer from each group to explain the layout, the information that has been included and what they think has been left out. Note any differences and similarities between the books.

Assessment

Pose a question related to the book's subject content.
Let the children identify the contents and index where to search for the information in the book.
Ask the children to question a partner about using the contents and index to find the information needed to answer their question.
Refer back to the learning outcomes on page 125.

Further work

Direct the children to the glossary of a classroom information book. Ask them to consider the words included.
Suggest they read a chapter of the book and identify words they would like to add. Can they identify the places for these additional entries in the book's glossary?

DAY 1 ■ Finding out more

Key features	Stages	Additional opportunities
	Introduction Before the lesson, check the websites you plan to use (see Independent work, below). Display the questions posed on Phase 1, Day 1. Ask the children: *How should I find the answers?* (Look in the appropriate place in an appropriate book.) Open and read aloud *The Great Fire of London* from the CD-ROM.	**Phonics:** f*ire*, wh*ere*, st*art* **HFW:** when, who, where, what
Information processing: identify relevant information from a range of sources on paper and on screen **Communication:** work collaboratively in whole-class contexts	**Independent work** Let the children re-read the text with their partners to identify where a question is answered. Demonstrate making simple notes (not sentences) near your question. Emphasise using your own words, but copying names accurately. Leave some questions unanswered. Ask the children: *Where else can I look?* Agree to use the internet. Investigate a relevant website together. For example www.tlfe.org.uk/clicker/flashhistoryks1/fireofLondon.swf. Discuss the website's layout and organisation. Are there hyperlinks? How do they work? As you investigate the text, demonstrate and discuss identifying key words. Does this allow you to scan rather than read closely? Model adding notes to your previous notes.	**Support:** a differentiated version of *The Great Fire of London* is available on the CD-ROM **Note:** the hyperlink from the suggested website links to a text box containing language that you may consider to be inappropriate for your class
	Plenary Discuss the two sources of information – book and ICT text. Which did the children find more useful?	

DAY 2 ■ Using the internet

Key features	Stages	Additional opportunities
	Introduction Make computers with internet access available to pairs of children. Remind the children of their partner discussion on Phase 1, Day 1 when they prepared questions about the Great Fire of London.	**Phonics:** f*ire*, wh*ere*, st*art* **HFW:** when, who, where, what
	Speaking and listening Let partners talk to each other as they consider if they want to add questions. Come together as a class, and remind the children of the importance in simple notes of using correct names and identifying key words.	
Information processing: identify relevant information from a range of sources on paper and on screen	**Independent work** Let the children, working in pairs, investigate yesterday's website (or a different one) making notes when they find answers to their questions. Offer support, helping individuals to keep their notes simple and clear. Point out that they may find an additional piece of information they particularly want to record.	**Support:** children can be helped with reading by a stronger partner
Evaluation: present information orally	**Plenary** Hold a progress report. Did the children's ICT research go well? Ask the children to make oral reports from their notes.	

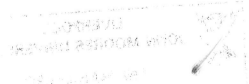

Key features	Stages	Additional opportunities
	### Introduction	**Phonics:** wom*a*n, v*oi*ce
	Introduce a new history topic. Without revealing the woman's name, show the children the photograph of Florence Nightingale from the CD-ROM. Do any of the children recognise the photograph? Do they know who she is?	**HFW:** when, who, where, what
Communication: develop their ability to listen critically to broadcast information and to make an oral presentation	### Speaking and listening	
	Play the recording of Florence Nightingale's voice from the CD-ROM. Let the children share their thoughts about the recording. Can they make out what Florence Nightingale is saying? Why do they think it sounds crackly?	
	Let partners share any information they have on Florence Nightingale. Have they heard of her? Who was Florence Nightingale? Are they sure of their facts?	
	Share ideas orally. Suggest that the children need more information. Encourage them to discuss with their partners what they want to find out.	
Enquiry: ask questions arising from work in another area of the curriculum	### Independent work	
	Give out copies of photocopiable page 138 'Florence Nightingale' for the children to list about six questions they want to pose.	
	Point out the usefulness of *Who? What? Where? When? What?* and *How?* as starting words.	
	### Plenary	
	Discuss the range of questions. Do the children think information will be hard to find? Save the questions for the next Phase.	

Guided reading

Let the children read *The Great Fire of London* from the CD-ROM. Working in a small group with your teaching assistant, ask them to identify the text's most important points. (For example, location of the fire; time of the fire; causes and consequences of the fire.) Extend the findings to a class discussion.

Assessment

Give the children a copy of *Florence Nightingale* from the CD-ROM. Question the children about the text. Ask: *What information in the text would you want to make a note of? What form and wording would your notes take?* A differentiated version of this text is available.
Refer back to the learning outcomes on page 125.

Further work

Following on from the assessment activity, challenge the children to make simple notes from the *Florence Nightingale* text from the CD-ROM. The children could show their notes to a partner. Does the partner find the information helpful?

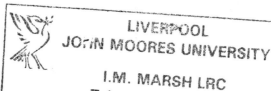

DAY 1 ■ Investigating websites

Key features	Stages	Additional opportunities
	Introduction Provide computers with internet access for the children. Check the websites you plan to use before the lesson. Remind the children of their questions about Florence Nightingale from Phase 2, Day 3. Suggest beginning their search for answers with a website. For example: www.bbc.co.uk/schools/famouspeople/standard/nightingale.	**Phonics:** nurse, good, note **HFW:** want, who, when
Enquiry: ask questions arising from work in another area of the curriculum	**Speaking and listening** Let the children remind themselves of their questions and discuss them with their partners. Come together as a class, and remind the children of the importance of simple notes, correct names, and identifying key words as they scan text for the information they want. Demonstrate these skills.	
Information processing: identify relevant information from a range of sources on screen	**Independent work** Let the children, working in pairs, investigate the website, making notes when they find information they want. Encourage the children to keep their notes simple and clear, Point out that they may find an additional piece of information they particularly want to record.	**Support:** children ask others to read text from screen; receive adult support with content and style of notes
	Plenary Hold a progress report. Is the children's research going well? Save questions and notes for the next day.	

DAY 2 ■ Evaluating reference books

Key features	Stages	Additional opportunities
	Introduction Collect a range of non-fiction books containing information about Florence Nightingale. Try to find a variety of books including: general history books, topic-specific books, encyclopedias. Put a selection of books on each table.	**Phonics:** nurse, note **HFW:** want, who, when
	Speaking and listening Encourage children to discuss yesterday's work with their partners. Do they have some questions still unanswered? Does some of yesterday's information need more detail?	
Information processing: identify relevant information from a range of sources on paper	**Independent work** Let the children continue with their notes from yesterday. Remind them to begin by evaluating a book's usefulness to them by skim-reading its title, contents page, illustrations, chapter headings and subheadings. What do these suggest the text will be about? Is the text likely to be useful?	**Support:** children have support with reading a text of an appropriate level
	Plenary Discuss the difference between ICT texts and books. Which day's research has been more profitable?	

DAY 3 ■ Continuing the research

Key features	Stages	Additional opportunities
	Introduction Discuss the progress of the children's research. Point out that the children's notes will inform their future writing, so they need to collect ample information about Florence Nightingale.	**Phonics:** *nurse*, *note* **HFW:** *where*, *what*
	Speaking and listening Let the children discuss problems they have met with their partners. Are there words they have not understood? Do they need help with a dictionary?	
Information processing: identify relevant information from a range of sources on paper	**Independent work** Organise groups as yesterday. Give each table a new selection of books. Remind them to copy names correctly and to note headings, key words and phrases that may be useful.	**Support:** point out questions the children still need to answer
	Plenary Ask the children: *Have the books surprised you? Is the information well organised?*	

DAY 4 ■ Evaluating resources

Key features	Stages	Additional opportunities
	Introduction Let the children finish making their notes. Is there something they could not find out? Have they considered asking someone else?	**Phonics:** *nurse*, *note* **HFW:** *night*, *good*
Evaluation: present information orally and in writing	**Speaking and listening** Does either partner have a problem? Can the other person help? Let partners compare progress and their attitudes to the resources. Have they been useful?	
	Independent work Give out copies of photocopiable page 139 'Useful sources'. Ask the children to evaluate the usefulness of resources they have used by completing the sheet.	
Communication: work collaboratively in paired and whole-class contexts	**Plenary** Listen to the children's views as you compare results. Which material proved most popular? Which information was easiest to access? Which was most useful?	

Guided reading

Guide the children as they read one of the *Florence Nightingale* texts from the CD-ROM with a partner.
Suggest that they identify the most important points and then share and compare findings with their group.

Assessment

Give the children the *Florence Nightingale* text from the CD-ROM. Ask them to make simple notes on two points in the text.
Refer back to the learning outcomes on page 115.

Further work

Using the knowledge they have gained from their research, ask the children to role play a conversation between Florence Nightingale and a soldier at the hospital.

DAY 1 ▪ Making a folding book

Key features	Stages	Additional opportunities
Enquiry: plan how to present information effectively	**Introduction** Remind the children of their interest in Florence Nightingale (see, Sequence 1 of this Unit). Show them examples of the books they used for research. Explain that you want them to create their own books about Florence Nightingale. **Speaking and listening** Let the children compare ideas with their partners on how to create and plan a book. Share ideas as a class. Suggest that decisions about the cover may often be left until last, but that writers plan a book's contents before they start writing. Revise the position and format of the contents page by displaying 'What's in the book?' from the CD-ROM. Demonstrate how to fold a piece of paper to create a simple, folding (concertina) book. **Independent work** Give out paper for the children to fold to make their books. They must plan in rough and then write their contents page including three or four chapter or section titles. They can complete page numbers later. **Plenary** Compare contents pages. Talk about pictures. Will only some chapters be illustrated?	**Phonics:** g*a*le, wh*ere* **HFW:** night, where **Support:** children work with a partner

DAY 2 ▪ The first chapter

Key features	Stages	Additional opportunities
Information processing: write their own information texts **Communication:** communicate outcomes in writing	**Introduction** Remind the children of their notes from Sequence 1 of this Unit. Write a few of your bulleted notes on the board and read them out. For example: ■ Who? *Nurse; British; cared about poor sick people.* Explain your first chapter will be called *Who was Florence Nightingale?* **Speaking and listening** Let the children discuss with their partners how you can create good text from your notes. Do they think you should add an illustration? Come together as a class, share ideas and demonstrate how to convert your notes into completed sentences. Encourage the children to contribute to sentence construction, vocabulary and spelling. **Independent work** Ask the children to check their notes for their first chapter, and then decide an the wording of sentences. Encourage them to rehearse wording (in their heads or with a partner) before writing the chapter heading and text. Would a picture and caption be useful? **Plenary** Compare chapter titles and talk about illustrations.	**Phonics:** n*u*rse, n*o*te **HFW:** who, was, people **Support:** children construct sentences orally with a partner before writing

DAY 3 ■ Continuing the books

Key features	Stages	Additional opportunities
	Introduction Return to yesterday's work. Emphasise the need for children to use their notes carefully. Are they spelling names correctly?	**Phonics:** nurse, note **HFW:** where, what
Information processing: write their own information texts **Communication:** communicate outcomes in writing	**Independent work** Let the children continue to write the text of their chapters. Encourage them to rehearse wording (in their heads or with a partner) before writing. Remind them to think about illustrations, perhaps leaving spaces to add them later.	
	Plenary Review the children's progress. Are they finding their notes clear? Emphasise that they will be able to spend more time on their books in the next Phase.	**Support:** children construct sentences with a partner

Guided reading

Give the children copies of *Common wild flowers* from the CD-ROM. Ask them to read it in pairs with support from your teaching assistant. Suggest that they discuss its layout and ways they could improve it.

Assessment

Let the children read *Common wild flowers* from the CD-ROM with a partner. Ask them to make brief notes individually. They should then find out if their partner's notes are useful by using them to construct a sentence. Refer back to the learning outcomes on page 125.

Further work

Ask the children to pretend they are writing a book called *Plants in the local environment* and to write the headings for the chapters they will include.

DAY 1 ■ Completing the books

Key features	Stages	Additional opportunities
	Introduction Return to the books that the children were writing in Sequence 2, Phase 1.	**Phonics:** nurse, note **HFW:** who, was, people
	Speaking and listening Use partner discussion as the children review their progress. Are all the chapters written? What about pictures and diagrams? Do they need captions and labels?	
Information processing: write their own information texts **Communication:** communicate outcomes in writing	**Independent work** Let the children complete their chapters and, when they are ready, move on to illustrations. Once the chapters are written, the children will be able to enter their page numbers in the contents list. Point out that the number entered should be the number of the page where the chapter starts.	**Support:** children keep writing brief
	Plenary Remind the children about the website you used (see Sequence 1, Phase 2). Look together at some pages. Discuss their layout. What makes a website's information useful and clear?	

DAY 2 ■ Designing a website

Key features	Stages	Additional opportunities
	Introduction As a class, investigate more fully the website on Florence Nightingale you used in Sequence 1, Phase 2. Point out the important features of website design: layout, text, diagrams and pictures, hyperlinks. Suggest that the children could make their books even more useful if they included a reference to a website, their own website.	**Phonics:** nurse, note **HFW:** who, was, people
Enquiry: plan how to present information effectively	**Speaking and listening** Encourage the children to share ideas with a partner for how they could design a website to link with part of their books.	
Communication: work collaboratively in paired contexts	**Independent work** Let the children work with a partner to create a design for a website. They should each make their own copy of the design. Encourage them to keep the design simple. Remind them that simple websites are easier to use.	
	Plenary Discuss any problems the children encountered. What difficulties do they foresee when they put the design into practice?	

DAY 3 ■ Creating a website

Key features	Stages	Additional opportunities
	Introduction You will need access to a computer for each pair of children. Remind them about yesterday's work as website designers, explain that they are now going to create the websites. (Programs such as Microsoft Word allow you to produce simple web pages – see 'Create a web page' in Microsoft Word Help.)	**Phonics:** nurse, note **HFW:** who, was, people
	Speaking and listening Suggest that the children review and discuss their design with their partner. Are any changes needed? Come together as a class. Emphasise the benefits of a clear straightforward website.	
Information processing: write their own information texts	**Independent work** As partners create their websites, encourage them to be willing to modify their ideas if they prove too complicated. Remind them that when they have used websites, they have preferred ones that are easy to use and are useful because the information is clear.	**Support:** children keep to a simple design **Extend:** encourage children to add hyperlinks and other features
Evaluation: judge effectiveness of their own work	**Plenary** Ask partners to report back on their experiences, presenting some features of their websites.	

Guided reading

Give out *Common wild flowers* from the CD-ROM for the children to read, with a partner or group and an adult. Suggest that they discuss words to include in the glossary and/or index.

If there is time, the children could progress to making their glossary or index.

Assessment

Tell the children that you would like them to plan a website to complement the *Common wild flowers* text.

Let the children think about the likely content. Ask:

- What text would it have?
- What features?
- How would it be different from paper information?

Refer back to the learning outcomes on page 125.

Further work

Expand the assessment work by letting the children put their website design on paper.

Suggest they present it to a partner. Does their partner think the information would be helpful?

DAY 1 ■ Adding a glossary

Key features	Stages	Additional opportunities
	Introduction Display the 'What's in the book' interactive activity from the CD-ROM. Point out *Glossary*. Ask the children: *What is it? How is it organised?* Suggest that the children should add a short glossary or list of special interest words to their book.	**Phonics:** short, how **HFW:** what, how
Information processing: write their own information texts	**Independent work** Encourage the children to read their book, asking themselves: *Which words are of special importance to the subject? Which would the reader want defined?* They should make a draft list and then arrange them in alphabetical order. Have an alphabet on display. Encourage the children to check partners' alphabetical order. Under the heading *Glossary* or *Special interest words*, ask the children to copy the list into their books and define the words.	**Support:** give children an alphabet line
	Plenary Share some glossary entries. Is the same word appearing frequently in different children's lists? Why is this quite likely? (The same area of study.)	

DAY 2 ■ Creating an index

Key features	Stages	Additional opportunities
	Introduction Ask the children to look carefully at their books.	**Phonics:** page, how **HFW:** what, how
	Speaking and listening Let partners discuss what they think is still missing from their books. Come together as a class and show and read aloud part of the index on the final page of a classroom book. Ask the children: *What do you notice?* (Alphabetical order; page numbers; sometimes more than one page number for the same word.) Emphasise the need for page numbering in their books.	
Information processing: write their own information texts	**Independent work** Ask the children, to decide on and make a draft list of words for their index. They must then arrange them in alphabetical order. Encourage children to ask a partner to check their alphabetical order before they copy the lists into books and add page numbers.	**Support:** give children an alphabet line
	Plenary Ask the children: *Have you thought about your book's cover?* Discuss some ideas.	

DAY 3 ■ Finishing touches

Key features	Stages	Additional opportunities
	Introduction Tell the children that their editorial deadline is today! List jobs on the whiteboard that they may still need to do. For example: *create a book cover; check all diagrams and pictures; add a reference to your website* (perhaps through the addition of a page footnote); *underline in the text the words in your glossary.*	**Phonics:** *name* **HFW:** *your, name*
Evaluation: judge the effectiveness of their own work	**Independent work** Let the children get busy! Remind them that the cover needs to show the author's name. Is their website complete? Encourage the children to have a final read. Are they pleased with their finished product?	**Extend:** children compare their books with texts they have used; is their information easy to find?
	Plenary Ask children to show the rest of the class their covers. What do the others learn and expect from them?	

DAY 4 ■ Evaluating the book

Key features	Stages	Additional opportunities
	Introduction If possible, provide computer access.	**Phonics:** *nurse, note* **HFW:** *who, was, people*
Evaluation: give feedback to others	**Speaking and listening** Invite the children to read their partners' books before supplying each other with oral feedback. What information was most useful? Were pictures helpful? Did they need the glossary often? Bring pairs together into fours for a wider readership. If possible, let the children demonstrate their websites.	
	Independent work Give out copies of photocopiable page 140 'Evaluation' for the children to complete about their own book.	
Evaluation: judge the effectiveness of their own work	**Plenary** Discuss what the children have learned from making a non-fiction book. Which pages were they most pleased with? How would most children plan to improve next time? Plan a visit by Year 1 children. Will they find answers to their questions about Florence Nightingale?	

Guided reading
Working in small groups, supported by your teaching assistant. Provide opportunities for the children to read two of the books by other children.
Ask them to report orally how they found them useful.

Assessment
Use the 'Plants glossary' interactive assessment activity from the CD-ROM. Ask the children to suggest the correct order for the words.
Refer back to the learning outcomes on page 125.

Further work
Ask the children to plan a new drag and drop activity featuring more plant words. They need to decide which plant words to use and write their meanings.

Florence Nightingale

NON-FICTION ■ UNIT 3

| Who?   Why?   When?   Where? |
| What?   How? |

_____

_____

_____

_____

_____

_____

_____

Useful sources

I looked for information about _____

I used these books: _____

_____

_____

I used these Internet websites: _____

_____

_____

The most interesting information I found was _____

_____

_____

The most useful source of information was _____

_____

_____

It was the most useful because _____

_____

_____

NON-FICTION ■ UNIT 3

Evaluation

How did readers react to the cover? _____

_____

_____

Which chapter was most popular and why? _____

_____

_____

How much were the glossary and index used? _____

_____

_____

Did readers comment on anything else? _____

_____

_____

How could you improve your next information book? _____

_____

NON-FICTION
UNIT 4 Non-chronological reports

Speak and listen for a range of purposes on paper and on screen

Strand 1 Speaking
■ Explain ideas and processes using imaginative and adventurous vocabulary and non-verbal gestures to support communication.

Read for a range of purposes on paper and on screen

Strand 5 Word recognition: decoding (reading) and encoding (spelling)
■ Read independently and with increasing fluency longer and less familiar texts.
■ Spell with increasing accuracy and confidence, drawing on word recognition and knowledge of word structure and spelling patterns.
■ Know how to tackle unfamiliar words which are not completely decodable.
■ Read and spell less common alternative graphemes including trigraphs.
■ Read high and medium frequency words independently and automatically.
Strand 6 Word structure and spelling
■ Spell with increasing accuracy and confidence, drawing on word recognition and knowledge of word structure and spelling patterns including common inflections and use of double letters.
■ Read and spell less common alternative graphemes including trigraphs.
Strand 7 Understanding and interpreting texts
■ Draw together ideas and information from across a whole text, using simple signposts in the text.
■ Explain organisational features of texts, including alphabetical order, layout, diagrams, captions, hyperlinks and bullet points.
Strand 8 Engaging with and responding to texts
■ Explain their reactions to texts, commenting on important aspects.

Write for a range of purposes on paper and on screen

Strand 9 Creating and shaping texts
■ Select from different presentational features to suit particular writing purposes on paper and on screen.
Strand 10 Text structure and organisation
■ Use planning to establish clear sections for writing.
■ Use appropriate language to make sections hang together.
Strand 12 Presentation
■ Word-process short narrative and non-narrative texts.

Progression in non-chronological reports

In this year, children are moving towards:
■ After a practical activity or undertaking some research in books or on the web, taking part in a discussion in another curriculum subject, generalising from repeated occurrences or observations.
■ Assembling information on another subject and using the text as a template for writing a report on it, using appropriate language to present and categorise ideas.

▶

UNIT 4 ◄ Non-chronological reports *continued*

Key aspects of learning covered in this Unit

Enquiry
Children will ask questions arising from work in another area of the curriculum, for example on teeth and eating, research and then plan how to present the information effectively.

Information processing
Children will identify relevant information from a range of sources on paper and on screen and use this to write their own non-chronological reports.

Evaluation
Children will present information orally and in writing. They will discuss success criteria, give feedback to others and judge the effectiveness of their own work.

Communication
Children will develop their ability to discuss as they work collaboratively in paired, group and whole-class contexts. They will develop their ability to listen critically to broadcast information and to make an oral presentation. They will also communicate outcomes in writing.

Prior learning

Before starting this Unit check that the children can:
■ Scan texts for information.
■ Offer opinions about the suitability of a text for research.
If they need further support please refer to a prior Unit or a similar Unit in Year 1.

Resources

Phase 1:
Going to school in Victorian times by David Waugh ✇; *Victorian outdoor games* by David Waugh ✇; Photocopiable page 153 'Evaluation grid'; Interactive activity 'Going to school in Victorian times' ✇; Interactive activity 'Victorian outdoor games' ✇

Phase 2:
Photocopiable page 154 'Writing skeleton'; Photocopiable page 155 'Feedback comments'; Non-chronological reports skeleton ✇

Phase 3:
Photocopiable page 156 'Victorian toys'; Interactive activity 'Going to school in Victorian times' ✇; Interactive activity 'Modern indoor play' ✇

Cross-curricular opportunities

History – Toys in the past

UNIT 4 ■ Teaching sequence

Phase	Children's objectives	Summary of activities	Learning outcomes
1	I can recognise a non-chronological report. I can use the text layout features to find information. I can ask and answer all my own questions based on the report. I can create a text map. I can use success criteria to evaluate different texts.	Read and analyse a non-chronological report. Identify the main features and retrieve specific information from a non-chronological report. Use an evaluation grid; identify reading pathways to retrieve information. Create a text map of a non-chronological report. Sort paper and ICT texts into more or less effective, using class success criteria.	Children can identify the main features of a non-chronological report, including grammatical features and key vocabulary. Children can evaluate non-chronological reports, expressing their views clearly and using evidence from the text.
2	I can read a writing skeleton. I can plan and create a skeleton. I can evaluate other skeletons. I can use feedback to edit my own skeleton.	Plan a skeleton of key interests. Plan and create a skeleton. Review, evaluate and give feedback on a draft plan. Read feedback comments and edit a plan appropriately.	Children can organise their ideas into general themes, subheadings, key details and information.
3	I can use my plans to write a topic paragraph. I can use a report template. I can write my own non-chronological report. I can edit text electronically. I can evaluate my partner's text. I can use feedback to edit my own report.	Collaborate on modelled writing. Write on a report template. Collaborate on revising and re-drafting text on screen. Give and receive oral feedback. Independently edit texts, addressing feedback points.	Children can write a paragraph on a theme, using subheadings, key details and information to structure the text.

Provide copies of the objectives for the children.

DAY 1 ▪ A journey through time

Key features	Stages	Additional opportunities
	Introduction Explain that the children are going to take a time travel journey into the past. Identify the destination by marking the Victorian age on a timeline. Explain that they are going to learn about how children lived then. Display and read aloud *Going to school in Victorian times* from the CD-ROM.	**Phonics:** inst*ea*d, t*au*ght **HFW:** school, would
Enquiry: ask questions arising from work in another area of the curriculum **Information processing:** identify relevant information from a range of sources on paper	**Independent work** Give the children copies of the text, asking them to re-read and discuss it with a partner. The children need to prepare oral answers, making notes to help them. Write on the whiteboard: ■ *Which word seems important in this text? How can you tell?* ■ *How is the text divided up?* ■ *What would be another possible order for the paragraphs? Does it matter?* ■ *Which paragraph needs to stay in the same place? Why?* **Plenary** Share the children's results, concluding that *Victorian* is a key word, this is obvious because of its repetition. Confirm that paragraphs can be in any order, but the first, introductory paragraph must remain as an opening. Identify the text as a non-chronological report and define the term.	**Support:** children can work with an adult or a partner **Extend:** children search a history textbook or the internet for a text on the same theme

DAY 2 ▪ Finding out about Victorian lessons

Key features	Stages	Additional opportunities
	Introduction Display and re-read *Going to school in Victorian times* from the CD-ROM. Ask the children: *What text type is it?* Identify important features of a non-chronological report, including: paragraphs; an opening; key words; some longer sentences. Write on the board: *What was the Victorian lesson for PE?* Demonstrate how to find the answer via the section heading. Highlight *Lessons.*	**Phonics:** inst*ea*d, t*au*ght **HFW:** school, would
Enquiry: ask questions arising from work in another area of the curriculum **Information processing:** identify relevant information from a range of sources on paper	**Independent work** Give out sticky notes and copies of the text. Write additional questions on the whiteboard and let the children search for the answers with their partner. As the children find the answer to each question, they should mark with sticky notes the heading or key word that helped them. As a class, discuss the children's answers and compare how they retrieved the information. Return to the first question you found the answer to. Display photocopiable page 153 'Evaluation grid'. Demonstrate how to grade the text layout for finding this answer. Give out copies of the photocopiable page and ask the children to evaluate the layout effectiveness for each answer. Remind them to check their sticky markers. The should put their answers in the 'Text A' column. **Plenary** Compare the children's results. Did everyone find headings useful? Why?	**Support:** reduce the number of questions and length of text searched **Extend:** give additional questions

DAY 3 ■ Effective non-chronological reports

Key features	Stages	Additional opportunities
Evaluation: discuss success criteria	**Introduction** Revise yesterday's work. Ask the children: *What helped you to retrieve information?* Let the children refer to their evaluation grids as they quote evidence to support their opinions. From these layout elements, collaborate on a class list of success criteria for an effective non-chronological report. Display and read aloud *Victorian outdoor games* from the CD-ROM. Give the children copies of the text and sticky notes.	**Phonics:** mar*ble*, gr*ou*nd **HFW:** five, many
Enquiry: ask questions arising from work in another area of the curriculum **Information processing:** identify relevant information from a range of sources on paper	**Speaking and listening** Ask the children a question, the answer to which is in the text. Working with a partner children should search for the information and mark with sticky notes the feature (reading pathway) that leads them to finding it. Let partners re-read the text before they retrieve information for another question posed by you. Compare results. Discuss how they will fill in their evaluation grids. **Independent work** Ask the children to generate a question based on the text. Their partner should find the answer, identify the reading pathway and then fill in the 'Text B' column of their evaluation grid. **Plenary** Discuss the children's results. Ask: *Did you use a new type of reading pathway?* Amend your success criteria for an effective non-chronological report. Do pathways make reading easier? Which type is most effective?	**Support:** reduce number of questions and length of text searched **Extend:** give children additional questions

DAY 4 ■ Analysing the layout

Key features	Stages	Additional opportunities
	Introduction Display *Going to school in Victorian times* from the CD-ROM. Ask the children: *Was it easy to retrieve information from this text? What helped you?* Demonstrate how to use tracing paper or acetate to trace over the layout of the page, marking headings, text and large spaces.	**Phonics:** mar*ble*, gr*ou*nd **HFW:** five, many
	Speaking and listening Let the children exchange ideas with their partners on the information given by your tracing. Share their opinions, explaining that you have created a text map that shows where different elements of the text appear. Compare these elements with the class success criteria (Day 3).	
Communication: work collaboratively in paired and whole-class contexts	**Independent work** Give out copies of *Victorian outdoor games* from the CD-ROM and ask the children, individually or in pairs, to create a text map. Afterwards they should check it against the class success criteria. Is the map appropriate for an effective non-chronological report? **Plenary** Display and discuss some of the text maps. Do the maps contain the success criteria? Will the maps help the children to write their own non-chronological reports?	**Support:** children work with partners **Extend:** children suggest additions that could be made to texts in order to meet success criteria

DAY 5 ▉ Looking at ICT texts

Key features	Stages	Additional opportunities
	### Introduction	

Introduction
Point out that so far you have focused on *paper* non-chronological reports. Ask the children: *What other type could we read?* (ICT-based.)
Use the computer to open an Internet website with non-chronological information on Victorian childhood, for example: www.Victorians.asp-host.co.uk/etoys/home.htm Read and try out some of the eToys page.

Phonics: *toy, first*
HFW: six, out

Information processing: identify relevant information from a range of sources on screen

Speaking and listening
Let the children discuss with their partners new features that are not used in paper reports. Do the class success criteria need to be changed?
Share ideas and amend and annotate the success criteria.

ICT link: children can use the 'Going to school in Victorian times' and 'Victorian outdoor games' interactive activities on the CD-ROM to test what they have learned about the Victorians from the two reports

Independent work
Refer to the ICT text as Text C, and give out copies of *Going to school in Victorian times* (Text A) and *Victorian outdoor games* (Text B). Ask the children to discuss the three texts with a partner. How do the texts fare against the criteria? Which is best? Ask the children to put a ranking order on their individual whiteboards.
Using a new colour of sticky notes, let the children mark information in texts A and B that they find particularly interesting, and save the sheets for the next Phase.

Plenary
Compare the text rankings. Let individuals justify their ranking with reference to the success criteria. Widen the discussion by asking: *What have we learned to help us write an effective non-chronological report?*

Guided reading
Let the children read *Going to school in Victorian times* and *Victorian outdoor games* in small groups with your teaching assistant. Ask them to identify some main features of a non-chronological report. What helps the reader find information quickly?
Would they put the paragraphs in this order?

Assessment
Question the children about 'Going to school in Victorian times' or 'Victorian outdoor games' from the CD-ROM.
Ask: *Do you find the texts helpful? Do you think they are good non-chronological reports? Which do you prefer? Why? Is one text more effective than the other?*
Assess the children's ability to use text evidence to support their view that one is more effective than the other.
Refer back to the learning outcomes on page 143.

Further work
Suggest that the children try to improve either 'Going to school in Victorian times' or 'Victorian outdoor games' from the CD-ROM.
They could design a new layout for the text, or use a different way of organising and ordering the text. Ask them to evaluate the improvement they have made to the text's effectiveness.

DAY 1 ▪ Using writing skeletons

Key features	Stages	Additional opportunities
	Introduction Display and read aloud *Going to school in Victorian times* from the CD-ROM. Highlight your key areas of interest. Suggest that you could use a skeleton to record them. Display the Non-chronological report skeleton from the CD-ROM. Move between the two screens as you check your areas of interest and then record them in the skeleton.	**Phonics:** inst*ea*d, t*au*ght **HFW:** school, would
Information processing: identifying relevant information from a range of sources on paper	**Independent work** Give out copies of *Going to school in Victorian times* for partners to talk to each other about how they could enter their key interests into a skeleton. Let the children use photocopiable page 154 'Writing skeleton' to record their ideas.	**Extend:** children compare ideas with another pair
	Plenary Share ideas, perhaps creating some of the children's skeletons on screen.	

DAY 2 ▪ Planning reading pathways

Key features	Stages	Additional opportunities
	Introduction Suggest that a skeleton is a useful way to plan reading or writing pathways through a non-chronological report. Display an empty skeleton from the CD-ROM. Ask: *How does a writer begin? Which word comes first?* Demonstrate how to write a general categorisation or definition in the centre. Progress to putting subheadings in the circles, and adding finally key details and information in the outer areas.	**Phonics:** mar*ble*, gr*ou*nd **HFW:** five, many
Information processing: identifying relevant information from a range of sources on paper	**Speaking and listening** Give the children copies of *Victorian outdoor games* from the CD-ROM. Ask them to talk to each other about how they would enter their key interests into a skeleton.	**Extend:** children plan skeleton of own key interests
	Plenary Ask individuals to describe how their skeletons would look.	

DAY 3 ▪ General theme to specific detail

Key features	Stages	Additional opportunities
	Introduction Give each group a curriculum-linked theme. For example: house types, rooms, heating, building materials. Working in a group ask the children to, discuss what should go on the skeleton. What will be the pathway from general theme (centre) to specific detail (outer parts)?	**Phonics:** *h*ouse, *r*oom
Information processing: identifying relevant information from a range of sources on paper	**Independent work** Display the class success criteria from Phase 1 and give out copies of photocopiable page 154 'Writing skeleton'. Children should discuss their ideas in groups, then fill in and save their draft skeletons.	
	Plenary Share the children's opinions on using skeletons for planning. Are they an effective method?	

DAY 4 ■ Evaluating the skeletons

Key features	Stages	Additional opportunities
	Introduction Put the children into yesterday's groups. Ask them to check their skeletons. Are they happy with their planning? Suggest that each group exchanges skeletons with another group.	**Phonics:** pl*a*n, r*ea*d **HFW:** make, help
Evaluation: give feedback to others	**Independent work** Encourage the children to review and evaluate the other group's plans. Do the pathways and text organisation seem effective? Ask for written comments on photocopiable page 155 'Feedback comments', perhaps in the form of notes. Encourage the children to use the language of the class success criteria.	**Support:** children rehearse feedback orally before writing
	Plenary Create an example skeleton using the interactive version from the CD-ROM. Emphasise the reading pathways. Keep a copy.	

DAY 5 ■ Incorporating feedback

Key features	Stages	Additional opportunities
	Introduction Remind the children about yesterday's evaluation of the skeleton text plans of another group. Let the children return the draft plans to their owners. Suggest that yesterday's groups exchange skeletons with another group.	**Phonics:** pl*a*n, r*ea*d **HFW:** make, help
Evaluation: give feedback to others and judge effectiveness of own work	**Speaking and listening** Encourage the groups to give and receive oral feedback. **Independent work** Independently, ask the children to read and consider the feedback comments they have received and to edit their texts appropriately.	**Support:** children have adult or partner support
	Plenary Ask the children: *Was feedback helpful? What changes did you make?*	

Guided reading

Ask the children to read *Going to school in Victorian times* from the CD-ROM in a group with your teaching assistant. Let them discuss and answer these questions:
What were the writer's key areas of interest?
What were some of the details?

Assessment

Find out if the children can explain how to use a skeleton to show key interests from *Going to school in Victorian times.*
Refer back to the learning outcomes on page 143.

Further work

Let the children pretend to be the writers of *Going to school in Victorian times* and ask them to create a skeleton. They might find it interesting to compare the results with a partner.

DAY 1 From plans to text

Key features	Stages	Additional opportunities
	Introduction Remind the children of the skeleton plans they created in Phase 2. Display yours from Day 4. Ask: *What is my general theme? What is a specific detail? Have I planned pathways for the reader?* Explain that you are now going to convert the plan into an effective non-chronological report text.	**Phonics:** plan, topic **HFW:** way, make
Information processing: identify relevant information from a range of sources	**Independent work** Let the children exchange suggestions for one of your subheadings with their partners. Come together as a class and model how to take one subheading and create a topic paragraph. Use a computer to make later changes manageable. Choose another subheading. Ask the children to discuss its content what its paragraph should contain.	
	Plenary Share the children's ideas. Model how to write another paragraph, emphasising your pathways for the reader as you create links between general and detail. Save your text.	

DAY 2 Using the success criteria

Key features	Stages	Additional opportunities
	Introduction Remind the children of your writing from yesterday. Ask them: *How can I be sure that I am including effective features?* Refer to and display the class success criteria from Phase 1, Day 3. Remind the children of what the grammatical and language features mean. Read the first paragraph that you wrote yesterday.	**Phonics:** plan, topic **HFW:** way, make
Information processing: identify relevant information from a range of sources	**Speaking and listening** Working with a partner, ask the children to check if the success criteria have been applied. Come together as a class to share opinions. Display yesterday's second paragraph.	
	Independent work Give out copies of the success criteria. Let the children continue to discuss the writing from yesterday with their partner. Ask them to check that you have followed the criteria in the second paragraph. Do you need to make any changes?	**Support:** children concentrate on limited number of criteria
	Plenary Share the children's ideas and discuss proposed changes. Do the other children agree? Point out where you have included the success criteria.	

DAY 3 ■ Using a skeleton template

Key features	Stages	Additional opportunities
	Introduction Remind the children that you have been writing topic paragraphs. Review the process so far: ■ Plan text on a skeleton. ■ Use the skeleton to write the text. ■ Use the support of the class success criteria. Display the Non-chronological report skeleton from the CD-ROM.	**Phonics:** report, template **HFW:** help
Enquiry: plan how to present the information effectively	**Independent work** Use partner and then class discussion to talk about how to use the template. The skeleton is shown on the bottom of the screen and the space above can be used to write the text. Choose a new subheading from your skeleton. Suggest that you write this section of the report. Collaborate with the children to write a paragraph. **Plenary** Discuss your progress. Ask the children: *Is the skeleton template helpful?*	

DAY 4 ■ Beginning to write

Key features	Stages	Additional opportunities
	Introduction Talk about the plans the children made on Phase 2, Day 5. Explain that you want them to convert their plans into text. Put the children into the groups they worked in during Phase 2.	**Phonics:** report, template **HFW:** help
Enquiry: plan how to present the information effectively	**Speaking and listening** Working in groups, encourage the children to refresh their memories about their plans. Come together as a class as you demonstrate again how to use the skeleton to write from, reminding the children of your writing process yesterday. Provide computers for the children with a word-processing program.	
Information processing: write their own non-chronological reports	**Independent work** Let each child begin writing their own section of the group's non-chronological report on the computer. **Plenary** Ask the groups to report on their progress so far.	**Support:** encourage oral exchanges during writing

DAY 5 Reviewing progress

Key features	Stages	Additional opportunities
	Introduction Remind the children about yesterday's task.	**Phonics:** rep*o*rt, templ*a*te **HFW:** help
Communication: work collaboratively in group contexts	**Speaking and listening** Encourage them to review the progress of their group and advise one another.	
Information processing: write their own non-chronological reports	**Independent work** Using laptops or a computer suite, continue with yesterday's writing. Each child should write their own section of the group's non-chronological report directly into the skeleton template. Remind them to think about the class success criteria.	
	Plenary Ask the children: *What difficulties have you had?*	

DAY 6 Editing the text

Key features	Stages	Additional opportunities
	Introduction Display the class success criteria. Display some of the text you wrote on Day 3. Ask the children: *Have I applied the success criteria well?*	**Phonics:** rep*o*rt, templ*a*te **HFW:** help
Communication: work collaboratively in whole-class contexts	**Whole-class work** In shared writing, revise and re-draft your text on screen. Encourage the children to make suggestions as you apply the class success criteria. Edit the text electronically.	
	Plenary Ask the children: *What other changes do I need to make?*	

DAY 7 Using notes to write a report

Key features	Stages	Additional opportunities
	Introduction Remind the children of the process of creating text and applying the success criteria.	**Phonics:** w*ou*nd, tr*ai*n **HFW:** play, called, up
Information processing: write their own non-chronological reports	**Independent work** Give out copies of photocopiable page 156 'Victorian toys'. Explain that these notes have been prepared as a plan for a non-chronological report. Ask children to write up the report. Afterwards they should check which success criteria they have used.	
Evaluation: discuss success criteria	**Plenary** View and read some of the children's reports. Where are the success criteria evident?	

DAY 8 ■ Giving feedback

Key features	Stages	Additional opportunities
	Introduction Display the class success criteria and remind the children of how you revised and re-drafted the text you wrote.	**Phonics:** wound, train **HFW:** play, called, up
	Speaking and listening Put the children into pairs. Suggest they use each other as response partners. They should read each other's text on screen and then give oral feedback.	
Evaluation: give feedback to others	**Independent work** Let the children begin to edit their own work on screen, pausing to discuss feedback and improvement possibilities with their response partners.	**Support:** children concentrate on small amount of text
	Plenary Ask the children: *Is a reader's opinion helpful? Why?*	

DAY 9 ■ From plans to text

Key features	Stages	Additional opportunities
	Introduction Remind the children that they are now writing the final version of their non-chronological report. The writing must be effective.	**Phonics:** wound, train **HFW:** play, called, up
	Speaking and listening Let response partners remind each other of their suggestions.	
Evaluation: judge the effectiveness of their own work	**Independent work** Ask the children to keep in mind the feedback points and the class success criteria as they independently edit their texts.	**Support:** children work on a small amount at a time with adult reminders of what to do next
Evaluation: present information in writing	**Plenary** Share some of the finished texts. Do the readers find the structure and language, of the texts, effective?	

Guided reading

Give pairs of children the opportunity to read at least two of the class's reports from Day 7. Suggest they identify and discuss with their partner differences in layout and features. Come together in a group with adult support, and ask the children to report their findings.

Assessment

Use the photocopiable assessment activity 'Modern indoor play'. The children need to plan and write a report similar to the reports on Victorian toys, but about their own modern toys. Remind them to use subheadings and key details of information.
Refer back to the learning outcomes on page 143.

Further work

Following on from the assessment activity let the children read each other's plan. The response partners should give each other evaluation feedback. Suggest the children use the feedback to edit their texts accordingly.

Name _____ Date _____

Evaluation grid

Text A	Text B
Question	Question
1.	1.
2.	2.
3.	3.
4.	4.
Layout or text feature	**Layout or text feature**
Effectiveness (good/fair/poor)	**Effectiveness (good/fair/poor)**

Writing skeleton

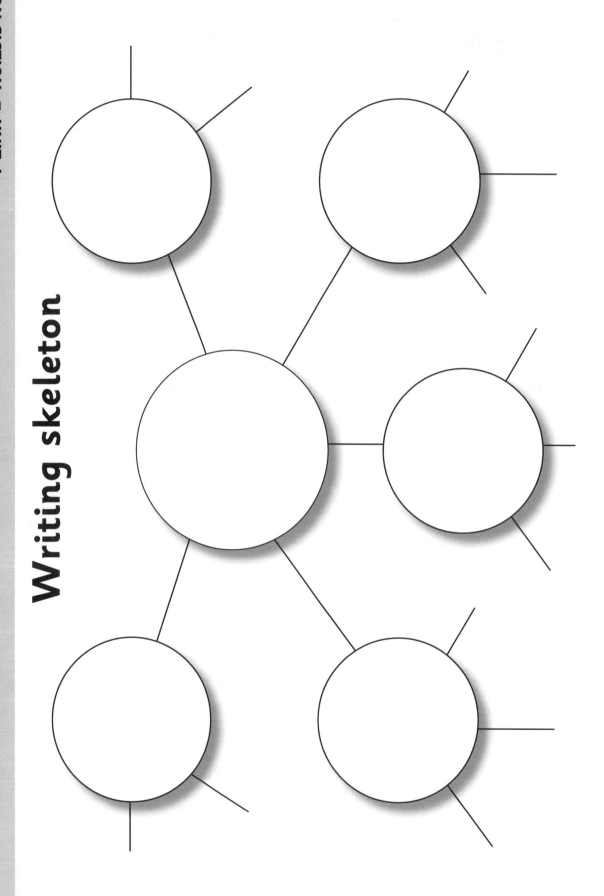

PHOTOCOPIABLE ■SCHOLASTIC
www.scholastic.co.uk

Feedback comments

Is the plan clear?_____

_____

What is good about the plan?_____

_____

What is difficult to understand?_____

_____

Can you follow the reading pathways?_____

_____

Are words in the best places?_____

_____

How would you improve the plan?_____

_____

Victorian toys

Jed has made notes for a non-chronological report. Help him out and write the report for him. Remember to write complete sentences and use some of the success criteria.

Jed's notes

- Books popular.

- Not allowed books or toys on Sunday; could only read Bible.

- Clockwork toys – had key to wind up.

- Clockwork toy train, wound up – went round track.

- Clockwork tin soldier – wound up, marched.

- Dolls popular, most made of cloth – called rag dolls.

- Some wooden – called Dutch dolls.

- Wax and china dolls – very expensive, only for rich.

_____

_____

_____

_____

_____

_____

_____

POETRY
UNIT 1 Patterns on the page

Speak and listen for a range of purposes on paper and on screen

Strand 1 Speaking
- Speak with clarity and use appropriate intonation when reading and reciting texts.

Strand 2 Listening and responding
- Respond to presentations by describing characters, repeating some highlights and commenting constructively.

Strand 3 Group discussion and interaction
- Ensure that everyone contributes, allocate tasks, and consider alternatives and reach agreement.
- Work effectively in groups by ensuring that each group member takes a turn challenging, supporting and moving on.
- Listen to each other's views and preferences, agree the next steps to take and identify contributions by each group member.

Strand 4 Drama
- Consider how mood and atmosphere are created in live or recorded performance .

Read for a range of purposes on paper and on screen

Strand 5 Word recognition: decoding (reading) and encoding (spelling)
- Read independently and with increasing fluency longer and less familiar texts.
- Spell with increasing accuracy and confidence, drawing on word recognition and knowledge of word structure and spelling patterns.
- Know how to tackle unfamiliar words which are not completely decodable.
- Read and spell less common alternative graphemes including trigraphs.
- Read high and medium frequency words independently and automatically.

Strand 6 Word structure and spelling
- Spell with increasing accuracy and confidence, drawing on word recognition and knowledge of word structure and spelling patterns including common inflections and use of double letters.
- Read and spell less common alternative graphemes including trigraphs.

Strand 7 Understanding and interpreting texts
- Explore how particular words are used, including words and expressions with similar meanings.

Strand 8 Engaging with and responding to texts
- Explain their reactions to texts, commenting on important aspects.

Write for a range of purposes on paper and on screen

Strand 9 Creating and shaping texts
- Draw on knowledge and experience of texts in deciding and planning what and how to write.
- Make adventurous word and language choices appropriate to the style and purpose of the text.
- Select from different presentational features to suit particular writing purposes on paper and on screen.

Strand 12 Presentation
- Write legibly, using upper and lower case letters appropriately within words, and observing correct spacing within and between words.
- Form and use the four basic handwriting joins

UNIT 1 ◀ Patterns on the page continued

■ Word-process short narrative and non-narrative texts.

Progression in poetry

In this year, children are moving towards:
■ Talking about own views, the subject matter and possible meanings; commenting on which words have most effect, noticing alliteration; discussing simple poetry patterns.
■ Performing individually or together; speaking clearly and audibly.
■ Making adventurous word choices to describe closely observed experiences.

Key aspects of learning covered in this Unit

Enquiry
Children will play games and ask questions about the patterns they can find in poems.
Reasoning
Children will explain the ways in which poems are patterned, and how those patterns could be continued or varied.
Evaluation
Children will discuss criteria for effective pattern poems, give feedback to others and judge the effectiveness of their word and presentational choices.
Communication
Children will begin to develop their ability to discuss patterns in the poetry and to create their own using carefully chosen words and phrases. They will sometimes work collaboratively in pairs and groups. They will communicate outcomes orally and in writing (possibly including ICT).

Prior learning

Before starting this Unit check that the children can:
■ Talk about favourite words or parts of a poem; notice a poem's pattern.
■ Perform in unison, following the rhythm and keeping time.
■ Imitate and invent actions.
■ List words and phrases or use a repeating pattern or line.
If they need further support please refer to a prior Unit or a similar Unit in Year 1.

Resources

Phase 1:
Samples of patterned carpets; *Shop Chat* by Libby Houston ❧; *Diamond Poem* by John Foster ❧; *The Shape I'm In* by James Carter ❧; Interactive activity 'A shape for a poem' ❧
Phase 2:
Sun's Day by Eileen Jones ❧; *Undersea Tea* by Tony Mitton ❧; *On the Ning Nang Nong* by Spike Milligan ❧
Phase 3:
Ten Things Found in a Wizard's Pocket by Ian McMillan ❧; *On the Ning Nang Nong* by Spike Milligan ❧; Photocopiable page 167 'Inside the wizard's pocket'; Photocopiable page 168 'The witch's shopping list'; Assessment activities 'Sound patterns' and 'Shape poem' ❧

Cross-curricular opportunities

Art and Design – Shape

UNIT 1 ■ Teaching sequence

Phase	Children's objectives	Summary of activities	Learning outcomes
1	I can identify patterns in poetry. I can plan and put on a poetry performance.	Identify sound, word and layout patterns. Plan and put on a performance with a partner. Make prose into a shape pattern poem. Add actions to a group recital.	Children can listen to, read and perform poems, identifying different patterns in their language use and structure
2	I can use words and expressions with similar meanings to create poems.	Explore patterns in shape poems. Write rain words for a class shape poem; choosing a shape. Write, with a partner, a line of the class rain poem.	Children understand how to play with interesting and inventive language choice to create or continue particular patterns. Children know how to go about writing a pattern or shape poem of their own.
3	I can use adventurous words and language to create patterns in poetry.	Explore structure patterns in a humorous poem. Add words and lines to a poem. Plan and write their own new poem.	Children can write a simple poem of their own, playing with interesting and inventive language choice to create or continue particular patterns.

Provide copies of the objectives for the children.

DAY 1 ■ What's in a pattern?

Key features	Stages	Additional opportunities
	### Introduction Ask the children to picture in their minds a carpet with a pattern on it. What do they see? Agree that their patterns differ, but that they all involve something repeated. If possible, show the children examples of some carpet patterns. Ask the children to listen for a pattern as you read aloud *Shop Chat* from the CD-ROM. Ask: *Which sounds are repeated in the poem's pattern? Which words? What effect do they have on the poem's meaning?*	**Phonics:** *shop, chat* **HFW:** *what, your*
Communication: discuss patterns in the poetry	### Speaking and listening Give out copies of *Shop Chat*. Let the children, in pairs, re-read it to each other. Ask them to discuss its sound patterns, underlining letters, phonemes or words that create the patterns. After 10 minutes, bring the class back together to share findings. Ask: *Which sounds are repeated in the poem's pattern? Which words? What effect do they have on the poem's meaning?*	
	### Independent work Ask the children to plan how to perform this poem with a partner. Suggest questions for them to consider: *Will you both speak every line? How can you best emphasise the poem's patterns?*	
	### Plenary Bring the class together. Discuss the rehearsals, and ask one person from each pair to explain their decisions. Listen to sample lines. Finish with a class performance in unison.	

DAY 2 ■ Layout patterns

Key features	Stages	Additional opportunities
	### Introduction Tell the children you have a shopping list on your kitchen noticeboard. Ask: *What does my list look like? How are the words written?* Agree that most lists are set out downwards, not across.	**Phonics:** *shop, chat* **HFW:** *what, your*
Enquiry: ask questions about the patterns they can find in poems	### Speaking and listening Give out copies of *Shop Chat* from the CD-ROM. Ask the children to hold partner discussions about its layout. What does it remind them of? Come together as a class and share ideas. Display *Shop Chat*. Point out that most of the poem is written like a list – a list of what is in the shop.	
	### Independent work Continue with yesterday's rehearsals. When the children are ready they can come together into fours. The pairs can take turns to act as performers and audience.	
	### Plenary Discuss the experience of performing and listening. Has it helped the children be more aware of the poem's patterns? Which words have stuck in their heads?	

DAY 3 ■ Make a shape

Key features	Stages	Additional opportunities
	### Introduction Display and read aloud the 'A shape for a poem' interactive activity from the CD-ROM. Question the children about its meaning. Ask: *What is being described? What is happening?* Draw the children's attention to some of the verbs used. Do they put pictures in the children's minds?	**Phonics:** *for, die, flame* **HFW:** red, into
Reasoning: explain the ways in which poems are patterned	### Speaking and listening Give each pair of children a copy of 'A shape for a poem' and ask them to discuss their reactions to the description. Can they identify patterns? Are there repeated sounds or words? Are lots of one type of word used? Encourage the children to listen to each other's views.	
	### Independent work Ask the children to become poets and write a poem of nine lines. Some lines will be very short. How will they divide it? Will they create a shape pattern to suit the meaning of the words? What title will they have? Some children could work on screen and use the interactive version of the resource; others can work on paper. All the children should keep their notes and designs for the next lesson.	
	### Plenary Discuss and highlight the patterns identified by the children. Let some children present their poem layouts by moving words about on screen. Do others find them effective?	

DAY 4 ■ Spot the shape

Key features	Stages	Additional opportunities
	### Introduction Return to 'A shape for a poem' from the previous day and some of the children's layouts. Point out sound and word patterns: *s, f,* repetition of *fire* and *flickers,* the list of action words. Finally reveal and discuss the poet's own layout. Can the children spot a shape pattern? Can they guess the chosen title before you reveal it? Show the children the true layout of the poem by displaying *Diamond Poem* from the CD-ROM.	**Phonics:** *shape, see* **HFW:** as, that, some
Communication: work collaboratively in groups	### Speaking and listening Put the children into small groups with copies of *The Shape I'm In* from the CD-ROM. Read it to the class. Ask the groups to plan performances of the poem. Ask: *Which lines will you say altogether? Which lines will be spoken individually? How will you emphasise words?*	**Support:** move between groups and give the children performance ideas if they need them
Communication: communicate outcomes orally and in writing	### Independent work Suggest the children add inventive actions. Ask them to draw or write their own ideas before re-joining their group. Ask the groups to consider ideas, reach decisions and rehearse their performances.	
	### Plenary Let the children present their performances. Encourage constructive discussion of them.	

Guided reading

Use the poems *Shop Chat, Diamond Poem* and *The Shape I'm In* from the CD-ROM for group reading with your teaching assistant.

Suggest the children work together, explaining the meaning of unusual words to one other.

Assessment

Use *Shop Chat* and *Diamond Poem* to assess the children's recognition of patterns in language and patterns in structure. Ask them to identify examples of each.

Refer back to the learning outcomes on page 159.

Further work

Extend the Assessment task by asking the children to read the two poems to a partner.

Let them compare their reactions to the poems. Do they both respond in the same way?

DAY 1 ■ Weather poems

Key features	Stages	Additional opportunities
	Introduction Display the poem *Sun's Day* from the CD-ROM and draw attention to its title. Ask the children: *Can you immediately see a pattern?* Read the poem aloud. Focus on small sections at a time, pointing out word, sound and structure patterns. Ask: *How is the poem divided? Are any sounds repeated deliberately? Is word sequence sometimes important?*	**Phonics:** *wake*, *share* **HFW:** time, about, out
Enquiry: ask questions about the patterns they can find in poems	**Speaking and listening** Using a section (about four couplets) of the poem, ask partners to take turns reciting them to each other. They should question each other: *Which line most made you think of the sun? Could you hear a special pattern in that line?*	
Communication: create their own poems using carefully chosen words and phrases	**Independent work** Explain that you want the children to plan a class poem called *Rain*. Ask the children to think of ideas for a special pattern in its layout. Suggest they sketch and write ideas on paper. Say that their final choice of layout, with three example rain words, should be ready to show the class in the plenary.	
	Plenary Ask the children to hold up their proposals. Encourage the children to look around. Are the ideas similar? Which ones remind them of rain? Begin a class collection of rain words.	

DAY 2 ■ Rain words

Key features	Stages	Additional opportunities
	Introduction Display and read aloud *Undersea Tea* from the CD-ROM.	**Phonics:** *sea*, *tea* **HFW:** there, very
Enquiry: ask questions about the patterns they can find in poems	**Speaking and listening** Ask the children to re-read it with a partner, considering questions about its shape pattern: *Why it is set out in this way? What does each line remind you of? Are vertical lines difficult to read?* Bring the class back together to share their opinions. Revise the children's work from the previous day. Remind them of your objective: to write a collaborative, class poem entitled *Rain*. Ask: *Which way should our lines read to look like rain?* Suggest vertical lines of raindrops.	
Communication: create their own poems using carefully chosen words and phrases	**Independent work** Ask the children to work, independently or with a partner, on some interesting rain words for the raindrops. Invite them to draw one or two raindrops on their individual whiteboards and write their favourite word(s) inside.	
	Plenary Compare the words that the children hold up. Add some to your class collection of rain words.	

DAY 3 ■ Experimenting with words

Key features	Stages	Additional opportunities
	Introduction Suggest to the children that a poet keeps experimenting with words. Read aloud some of *On the Ning Nang Nong*. Ask: *What is its special pattern?* (A list of noises; a repeated chorus.)	**Phonics:** *cow, where* **HFW:** *where, just*
Enquiry: ask questions about the patterns they can find in poems	**Speaking and listening** Ask pairs of children to exchange their views on this poem. What did they think of the words? Were they correct words? Why did the poet use them? Share the results of the partner discussions. Explain that poets sometimes invent words, creating expressive sound patterns. Suggest using unusual language in your *Rain* poem. Demonstrate creating an inventive line of raindrops. For example: *Rain can... Splish, splash, splosh.* (Write the words vertically on the board to look like raindrops.)	
Communication: create their own poems using carefully chosen words and phrases	**Independent work** Ask the children, with a partner, to write their downward line of words for the *Rain* poem. Suggest consonant clusters – *sw, dr, pl* – as useful word beginnings. Emphasise that some words may be invented. **Plenary** Collect a line of rain words from every pair of children, helping everyone to contribute. Continue to make improvements by collaborating on the best order for the lines. Finally, hold a grand performance.	**Support:** help the children by providing starting words. For example: *pitter, drip, plop, squelch*

Guided reading
Let small groups of children read *On the Ning Nang Nong* with adult support. Ask: *Which are nonsense/invented words? Why has the writer used them?* Ask the children to identify words that play with language, and words that continue particular patterns.

Assessment
Ask the children to think of some words and phrases that they might use if they were going to write a poem about the wind. They can include some invented words. They should also think about how their poem might appear on the page. Refer back to the learning outcomes on page 159.

Further work
Extend the assessment task by asking the children to discuss with a partner what other poems they could write that played with inventive language. What would the poem be about? What invented words would they use?

DAY 1 ■ Repeating patterns

Key features	Stages	Additional opportunities
	Introduction Display and read aloud *Ten Things Found in a Wizard's Pocket* from the CD-ROM. Do the children think it is a very serious poem? Ask: *Would a large elephant really fit in a pocket?*	**Phonics:** st*ar*, c*ar* **HFW:** some, ten
Enquiry: ask questions about the patterns they can find in poems	**Speaking and listening** Ask the children to discuss the poem with their partners. Ask them: *What does this poem look and sound like? What patterns can you find? Does the poem repeat words?* Bring the class back together to share their findings. Draw the children's attention to the structure pattern formed by the line beginnings.	
Communication: create their own poems using carefully chosen words and phrases	**Independent work** Individually or with partners, ask the children to decide on about four interesting items to add to the wizard's pocket. Use photocopiable page 167 'Inside the wizard's pocket'. Challenge them to try to put the items into four new lines for the poem.	
Evaluation: give feedback to others	**Plenary** Ask the children to read their writing to the class. Encourage the audience to comment constructively on language they have enjoyed. Draw their attention to imaginative vocabulary and make additional suggestions.	

DAY 2 ■ List poems

Key features	Stages	Additional opportunities
Reasoning: explain the ways in which poems are patterned and how those patterns could be continued	**Introduction** Remind the children of your kitchen noticeboard shopping list from Phase 1, Day 2. Ask: *What would my list look like as a poem?* (Quite long and quite thin.) Introduce a scenario: the witch, jealous of the wizard's exciting possessions, is writing a shopping list. Model on the board how she may have begun her list. Share ideas orally on how she may continue.	**Phonics:** st*ar*, m*oo*n **HFW:** one, two
	Speaking and listening Ask the children to talk to a partner about ideas for the witch's list. Emphasise the need for interesting, exciting items. Both partners will need to keep notes on what they decide to add.	
Communication: create their own poems using carefully chosen words and phrases	**Independent work** Ask the children, independently or with their partner, to work on writing a poem, based on the witch's shopping list. Remind them to experiment before deciding on the best words and to maintain the poem's pattern. Point out that the poem does not have to be finished today. Use photocopiable page 168 'The witch's shopping list' for this draft or tomorrow's final version.	**Support:** children can make notes by drawing items before they write
	Plenary Pretend that you have also been thinking about the witch's list. Share some ideas and demonstrate how to make improvements.	

DAY 3 ■ Playing with words

Key features	Stages	Additional opportunities
	### Introduction Display and read aloud *Ten Things Found in a Wizard's Pocket*. Point out imaginative choices. For example: *A snoring rabbit.* Remind the children about some of the inventive language of *On the Ning Nang Nong.* Suggest they can be equally playful with some of their words.	**Phonics:** st*ar*, c*ar* **HFW:** some, ten
Evaluation: judge the effectiveness of their word choices	### Speaking and listening Ask the children to return to the previous day's work. Suggest they read it to their partner, asking: *Could some words be more interesting? Could a sound or word pattern be made? Is this line in the best place?*	**Support:** provide children with a bank of vocabulary
	### Independent work Ask the children to finish and edit their drafts, before writing final, polished versions of the poems, by hand or computer.	**Extend:** let the children write a second, independent pattern poem with some repeated
Communication: communicate outcomes orally and in writing	### Plenary Allow ample time for the children to act as performers and audience as they listen to one another's presentations. Compile the poems in a class display, book or ICT presentation.	phrases or chorus lines

Guided reading

Help the to children read *On the Ning Nang Nong*. Suggest that they make a 'top three' list of the animals that sound most fun. They can then compare their list with their partner's and explain their choices. Encourage them to refer to the language of the poem.

Assessment

Give the children copies of the 'Sound patterns' and 'Shape poem' photocopiable assessment activities from the CD-ROM.
Refer back to the learning outcomes on page 159.

Further work

Progress from the Assessment task by providing the children with a manageable poetry anthology. (Perhaps limit their selections of pages to use.)
Can they identify a new poem with an interesting pattern?

Inside the wizard's pocket

_____

_____

_____

_____

Name _____ **Date** _____

The witch's shopping list

One giant giraffe.

Two toads to frighten the wizard.

_____

_____

_____

_____

_____

_____

_____

_____

Illustration © Nova Developments.

PHOTOCOPIABLE ■SCHOLASTIC
www.scholastic.co.uk

POETRY
UNIT 2 Really looking

Speak and listen for a range of purposes on paper and on screen

Strand 1 Speaking
- Speak with clarity and use appropriate intonation when reading and reciting texts.

Strand 2 Listening and responding
- Respond to presentations by describing characters, repeating some highlights and commenting constructively.

Strand 3 Group discussion and interaction
- Ensure that everyone contributes, allocate tasks, and consider alternatives and reach agreement.
- Work effectively in groups by ensuring that each group member takes a turn challenging, supporting and moving on.
- Listen to each other's views and preferences, agree the next steps to take and identify contributions by each group member.

Strand 4 Drama
- Consider how mood and atmosphere are created in live or recorded performance.

Read for a range of purposes on paper and on screen

Strand 5 Word recognition: decoding (reading) and encoding (spelling)
- Read independently and with increasing fluency longer and less familiar texts.
- Spell with increasing accuracy and confidence, drawing on word recognition and knowledge of word structure and spelling patterns.
- Know how to tackle unfamiliar words which are not completely decodable.
- Read and spell less common alternative graphemes including trigraphs.
- Read high and medium frequency words independently and automatically.

Strand 6 Word structure and spelling
- Spell with increasing accuracy and confidence, drawing on word recognition and knowledge of word structure and spelling patterns including common inflections and use of double letters.
- Read and spell less common alternative graphemes including trigraphs.

Strand 7 Understanding and interpreting texts
- Explore how particular words are used, including words and expressions with similar meanings.

Strand 8 Engaging with and responding to texts
- Explain their reactions to texts, commenting on important aspects.

Write for a range of purposes on paper and on screen

Strand 9 Creating and shaping texts
- Draw on knowledge and experience of texts in deciding and planning what and how to write.
- Make adventurous word and language choices appropriate to the style and purpose of the text.
- Select from different presentational features to suit particular writing purposes on paper and on screen.

Strand 12 Presentation
- Write legibly, using upper and lower case letters appropriately within words, and observing correct spacing within and between words.
- Form and use the four basic handwriting joins.

▶

■ Word-process short narrative and non-narrative texts.

Progression in poetry

In this year, children are moving towards:
■ Talking about own views, the subject matter and possible meanings; commenting on which words have most effect.
■ Performing individually or together; speaking clearly and audibly.
■ Making adventurous word choices to describe closely observed experiences.

Key aspects of learning covered in this Unit

Enquiry
Children will play games and ask questions about the descriptive detail they can find in poems.

Reasoning
Children will explain the ways in which poems show descriptive detail and how that descriptive detail could be continued.

Evaluation
Children will discuss criteria for effective descriptive detail poems, give feedback to others and judge the effectiveness of their word and presentational choices.

Communication
Children will begin to develop their ability to discuss descriptions in the poetry and to create their own using carefully chosen words and phrases. They will sometimes work collaboratively in pairs and groups. They will communicate outcomes orally and in writing (possibly including ICT).

Prior learning

Before starting this Unit check that the children can:
■ Listen to and follow a poem's message; notice a poem's words.
■ Perform in unison, following the rhythm and keeping time.
■ Imitate and invent actions; list words and phrases.
If they need further support please refer to a prior Unit or a similar Unit in Year 1.

Resources

Phase 1:
It's Spring by John Foster ✿; *Walking to School* by Stanley Cook ✿
Phase 2:
Print Out, Wipe Out by Trevor Harvey ✿; *Walking to School* by Stanley Cook ✿
Phase 3:
Willow Pattern by Tony Mitton ✿; Photocopiable page 179 'The Willow Pattern'; Photocopiable page 180 'In the park'; Photograph of a Willow Pattern plate ✿
Phase 4:
Flowers for children to observe and draw; Photographs of flowers ✿; Asessment activity 'An animal friend' ✿

Cross-curricular opportunities

Geography – Around our school
Art and Design – Exploring and developing ideas

UNIT 2 ■ Teaching sequence

Phase	Children's objectives	Summary of activities	Learning outcomes
1	I can comment on descriptions in poems. I can relate a poem to my own experiences.	Listen to a descriptive poem and analyse text with a partner. Relate a poem to direct experience. Create a description of their own similar experience.	Children can relate a poem's details to their own experiences.
2	I can bring a poem to life through dance and drama.	Plan and put on a group performance of a poem using dance and drama.	Children can respond to poetry through dance and drama.
3	I can respond to and use descriptive details in poetry.	Listen to a poem and record impressions. Write own detailed descriptions and see a poem modelled.	Children can recognise the careful selection of words.
4	I can write descriptive poetry after looking really closely at an object.	Produce a detailed description through a drawing. Capture the same detail in a descriptive poem.	Children can write a simple poem of their own, in response to direct observation.

Provide copies of the objectives for the children.

DAY 1 ▪ Poetry or prose?

Key features	Stages	Additional opportunities
	Introduction Explain to the children that you are going to read an account written by someone who had just realised that winter was over. Then read aloud *It's Spring* from the CD-ROM. Ask the children to imagine the words on the page. Display the poem. Ask: *Were you correct? Did you know it was a poem?* Point out that poems and pieces of prose description can say the same things. **Speaking and listening** Ask the children to share with a partner their first experience of noticing the arrival of spring. Did anything surprise them? What did they notice first? Bring the class back together and ask one person from each pair to say what their partner described.	**Phonics:** aw*ay*, p*u*ll **HFW:** now, then
Enquiry: ask questions about the descriptive detail they can find in poems	**Independent work** Ask the children, with a partner, to re-read the poem, investigating the form of the poem. Pose questions: *How is it divided up? What can you discover about line length? Does the poem have a pattern?* Which words tell them that the poet was looking closely at nature? **Plenary** Share the discussion results, reinforcing poetic vocabulary, line and verse. Point out that poets do not have to use rhyme. Read the poem together.	

DAY 2 ▪ Picture the journey

Key features	Stages	Additional opportunities
	Introduction Read aloud *Walking to School* from the CD-ROM. Ask the children: *Does it sound like a poem or a description?* Suggest that it sounds as if someone is describing their journey as they make it. Display the poem and read it aloud again. **Speaking and listening** Ask the children to re-read the first two verses with a partner, identifying the rhyme pattern. Which words makes the houses sound as if they are standing up straight? Share ideas as a class.	**Phonics:** p*oo*l, h*ou*se **HFW:** here, house
Reasoning: explain the way in which poems show descriptive detail	**Independent work** Read out the poem several more times and ask the children to decide and record (in drawing or writing) which three details of the journey they think are best described. Which words do they like because they paint vivid pictures in their minds? **Plenary** Compare the children's ideas. Agree that the poet looks carefully at everything.	

DAY 3 ◼ Describing landmarks

Key features	Stages	Additional opportunities
	Introduction Remind the children of the poem *Walking to School* from the CD-ROM. Describe in a similar way some of the things on your route to school. Ask the children to sketch their route (preferably by foot), marking their three favourite landmarks.	**Phonics:** pool, house **HFW:** here, house, who
Communication: develop their ability to discuss descriptions	**Speaking and listening** Ask the children to tell a partner about their landmarks. They need to think how they can best describe the landmarks in words so their partner imagines them vividly. Bring the class back together and listen to some descriptions. Make suggestions so that the children see how to improve and extend them. Ask the children to comment on a word that paints a vivid picture in their minds.	
Communication: create their own poetry using carefully chosen words and phrases	**Independent work** Ask the children to pretend they are still talking to their partner as they write a description, in prose or poetry, describing their journey landmarks. Encourage them to write poems in lines and perhaps verses, but not to use rhymes. **Plenary** Give everyone the opportunity to recite their poem to their partner and then a small group, before listening to some as a class.	**Support:** suggest starting words for the children's writing

Guided reading
Let the children read *Walking to School* in groups with your teaching assistant. Suggest they divide into pairs and split the poem up, with partners concentrating on two verses. Afterwards let them discuss their own journeys to school.

Assessment
Assess the children's awareness of descriptive details in a poem by asking them to read four verses of *Walking to School*.
Ask: *What four details are pointed out? Are there any similar details on your journey to school?*
Refer back to the learning outcomes on page 171.

Further work
Ask the children to read the other verses of *Walking to School*.
Ask: *What other details are pointed out? Which one is closest to your personal experience?*

DAY 1 ▪ Poetry in action

Key features	Stages	Additional opportunities
	### Introduction Read aloud, twice, *Print Out, Wipe Out* from the CD-ROM.	**Phonics:** *more*, *keen* **HFW:** old, one
Communication: develop their ability to discuss descriptions in the poetry	### Speaking and listening Ask the children to share ideas about its meaning with their partners. Discuss the meaning as a class. Ask: *Which word have you read in a recent poem to describe a row of houses?* (Parades.) *What does it describe here?* Demonstrate its appropriateness by typing a word.	
	### Independent work In groups of four, ask the children to plan how to bring the words to life, miming the actions of the poem as it is read. They must keep checking what the poet's computer is doing to ensure that their actions are correct.	**Support:** use dance and drama groupings of mixed abilities
	### Plenary Ask each group to choose a spokesperson to describe their plan.	

DAY 2 ▪ Using dance and drama

Key features	Stages	Additional opportunities
	### Introduction Display and read in unison *Print Out, Wipe Out* from the CD-ROM.	**Phonics:** *more*, *keen* **HFW:** old, one
Evaluation: judge the effectiveness of their presentational choices	### Speaking and listening Ask yesterday's groups to talk again about their planned actions and dance. Pose questions to consider: *What changes are needed? Should we add sounds (for example, a tapping noise)?* Emphasise the need for the groups to make decisions.	
Communication: work collaboratively in groups	### Independent work Allow rehearsal time before the children perform for another group.	
	### Plenary Read in unison, as each group has a turn at presenting its dance drama. Demonstrate bringing to life the poem's message with letters and words on screen. Make the finale a class performance directed by you.	

Guided reading
Give the children copies of *Print Out, Wipe Out* to read with a partner or group with adult support. Suggest they search the poem for action verbs. How many can they find? Which ones are most appropriate?

Assessment
Let the children read *Print Out, Wipe Out*. Can they describe to a partner how they brought each section to life through dance and drama? Refer back to the learning outcomes on page 171.

Further work
Encourage the children to relate the poem more closely to their own experience by attempting to make the poem's actions occur on a computer. Ask: *Are the descriptions in the poem realistic?*

DAY 1 ▪ The Willow Pattern

Key features	Stages	Additional opportunities
	Introduction Show the children the photograph of the Chinese Willow Pattern from the CD-ROM. Explain that it is traditional as a plate pattern and that the pattern tells a story.	**Phonics:** blue, bird **HFW:** man, there, blue
	Speaking and listening Ask the children to share ideas with their partners on what is happening in the pattern's story. Collect ideas from the class.	
Enquiry: ask questions about the descriptive detail they can find in poems	**Independent work** Give the children copies of photocopiable page 179 'The Willow Pattern'. Explain that they are going to listen to the story being read and that they need to record what is happening on the photocopiable page. Tell them that the story is in the form of a poem. Ask the children to listen carefully as you read aloud verses two to six of *Willow Pattern* from the CD-ROM. Allow plenty of time for the children to record what is happening in the boxes on the photocopiable page.	
	Plenary Ask the children to show and talk about their drawings. Discuss their reactions to the story. Display the poem and read it in unison.	

DAY 2 ▪ Picture the story

Key features	Stages	Additional opportunities
	Introduction Display and read the whole of *Willow Pattern* from the CD-ROM. Ask the children: *Is the first word important? How does it make you feel?*	**Phonics:** blue, bird **HFW:** man, there, time
Reasoning: explain the way in which poems show descriptive detail	**Speaking and listening** Ask the children to investigate the poem with a partner. Is there a rhyme pattern? Bring the class back together and agree that the poem does not have a rhyme pattern, but concentrates on describing detail. Point out detail and particularly effective verbs: *droops, weeps, fled*. These help them see the blue plate in their minds.	
	Independent work Give out photocopiable page 180 'In the park'. Ask the children to create a park plate containing a story, or a number of separate short stories. Afterwards, the children should imagine their plate is invisible to other people. Suggest they list effective adjectives or verbs that will help other people 'see' their plate.	**Support:** provide small bank of words as starting points
	Plenary Collect words from the children. Model how to put some of them into a poem, following the format of the *Willow Pattern* poem.	

Guided reading

Help the children to work in groups and read aloud *Willow Pattern*. Individuals or partners could take turns to read a verse and explain what they have just read.

Assessment

Assess the children's recognition of the benefit of careful selection of words by asking them to tell you the story/stories on their plate.
Select people or objects on the plate. Ask: *What would be effective words to help a reader 'see' them? What would those words make the reader think of?* Refer back to the learning outcomes on page 171.

Further work

Extend the assessment work by suggesting the children use their plates and effective words to write a poem, trying to follow the format of the *Willow Pattern* poem.

DAY 1 ■ Looking at details

Key features	Stages	Additional opportunities
	Introduction Set a flower on each table, perhaps one between each pair of children. Alternatively, use the photographs of the flowers on the CD-ROM. Explain that you want the children to draw a flower – with enough detail that it will still seem alive once you have to throw it away.	**Phonics:** dr*aw*, l*eaf* **HFW:** made, as
Communication: work collaboratively in pairs	**Speaking and listening** Ask the children to discuss the task with a partner, exchanging views on what they feel about drawing the flower and how it can best be made to look alive. Share views as a class. Agree on the need to reproduce details. Point out examples on the flower – such as the curl of a petal or the veins of a leaf.	
	Independent work Let the children do their drawings. Encourage partners to offer advice and mutual support. Emphasise that the children need to keep looking very closely at their flowers.	
	Plenary Offer praise. Point out examples of small detail, but try to find details of the flower in everyone's observational drawings.	

DAY 2 ■ An experience shared

Key features	Stages	Additional opportunities
	Introduction Remind the children of their flower drawings. Ask them to think about how they felt before and during the task.	**Phonics:** dr*aw*, l*eaf* **HFW:** made, after
	Speaking and listening Ask the children to share their thoughts with a partner. Encourage them to use words that will help their partner to share the experience.	
Communication: communicate outcomes in writing	**Independent work** Ask the children to write about their thoughts and feelings before, during and after drawing the flower. Writing can be either a prose description or a poem. Suggest doing the writing in three parts – before, during and after. You could provide these as starting words.	
	Plenary Ask the children to read their descriptions to a partner. Does the partner now have better understanding of their feelings? Ask them to say which words they found most helpful.	

DAY 3 ◗ A picture in words

Key features	Stages	Additional opportunities
	### Introduction Suggest that you would like children to write a poem that creates a 'picture' of the flower in words. People reading and listening to the words should be able to 'see' the flower without the picture or the flower being there. Emphasise the need for well-chosen words to supply this detail.	**Phonics:** shape, leaf **HFW:** with, after
Communication: discuss descriptions in the poetry	### Speaking and listening Ask the children to discuss language for their poems with a partner. What words and phrases can they think of? What words would best describe the colour? What about the shape? Suggest that the children may want to make notes.	
Communication: create their own poetry using carefully chosen words and phrases	### Independent work Ask the children to write their poems, independently or with their partners. Remind them that the readers should feel that they are really looking at the flower. Encourage the children to be adventurous in their language choice, and to treat their first writing as a draft before they write their final poem.	
	### Plenary Share the finished poems, encouraging everyone to read aloud to an audience. Ask the audience to close their eyes so the poem's words can work their magic.	

Guided reading

Working in groups with your teaching assistant, give the children the opportunity to read a poem that is written in response to direct observation. They could read their own flower poems to one another, or you could provide your copies of a poem such as *I Saw* by Anon from *The Works*, chosen by Paul Cookson (Macmillan). Encourage them to discuss the pictures made by the words.

Assessment

Let the children complete the 'An animal friend' photocopiable assessment activity from the CD-ROM. Let the children talk about the animal they will use.
Ask preparatory questions such as: *What does it look like? How does it sound and feel? What about its movement?*
A picture could be a good starting point.
Refer back to the learning outcomes on page 171.

Further work

Extend the assessment activity by asking the children to read their poems aloud to a partner. Encourage them to discuss their reactions to each other's words. Do the animals seem real?

Name ———————————————— **Date** ————————————

The Willow Pattern

1	
2	
3	
4	
5	

Name _____ **Date** _____

In the park

■ Use the pictures to create a modern plate design that tells a story set in a park.

■ 100 LITERACY FRAMEWORK LESSONS YEAR 2

PHOTOCOPIABLE ■ SCHOLASTIC
www.scholastic.co.uk

POETRY
UNIT 3 Silly stuff

Speak and listen for a range of purposes on paper and on screen

Strand 1 Speaking
- Speak with clarity and use appropriate intonation when reading and reciting texts.

Strand 2 Listening and responding
- Respond to presentations by describing characters, repeating some highlights and commenting constructively.

Strand 3 Group discussion and interaction
- Ensure that everyone contributes, allocate tasks, and consider alternatives and reach agreement.
- Work effectively in groups by ensuring that each group member takes a turn challenging, supporting and moving on.
- Listen to each other's views and preferences, agree the next steps to take and identify contributions by each group member.

Strand 4 Drama
- Consider how mood and atmosphere are created in live or recorded performance .

Read for a range of purposes on paper and on screen

Strand 5 Word recognition: decoding (reading) and encoding (spelling)
- Read independently and with increasing fluency longer and less familiar texts.
- Spell with increasing accuracy and confidence.
- Know how to tackle unfamiliar words which are not completely decodable.
- Read and spell less common alternative graphemes including trigraphs.
- Read high and medium frequency words independently and automatically.

Strand 6 Word structure and spelling
- Spell with increasing accuracy and confidence, drawing on word recognition and knowledge of word structure and spelling patterns including common inflections and use of double letters.
- Read and spell less common alternative graphemes including trigraphs.

Strand 7 Understanding and interpreting texts
- Explore how particular words are used, including words and expressions with similar meanings.

Strand 8 Engaging with and responding to texts
- Explain their reactions to texts, commenting on important aspects.

Write for a range of purposes on paper and on screen

Strand 9 Creating and shaping texts
- Draw on knowledge and experience of texts in deciding and planning what and how to write.
- Make adventurous word and language choices appropriate to the style and purpose of the text.
- Select from different presentational features to suit particular writing purposes on paper and on screen.

Strand 12 Presentation
- Write legibly, using upper and lower case letters appropriately within words, and observing correct spacing within and between words.
- Form and use the four basic handwriting joins.
- Word-process short narrative and non-narrative texts.

UNIT 3 ◄ Silly stuff *continued*

Progression in poetry

In this year, children are moving towards:
■ Talking about own views, the subject matter and possible meanings; commenting on which words have most effect, noticing alliteration; discussing simple poetry patterns.
■ Performing individually or together; speaking clearly and audibly; using actions and sound effects to add to the poem's meaning.
■ Experimenting with alliteration to create humorous and surprising combinations; making adventurous word choices to describe closely observed experiences; using simple repeating phrases or lines as models.

Key aspects of learning covered in this Unit

Enquiry
Children will play games and assess how funny language can be in poems.
Reasoning
Children will explain the ways in which language is humorous.
Evaluation
Children will find ways to use language playfully, give feedback to others and judge the effectiveness of their word and presentational choices.
Communication
Children will begin to develop their ability to discuss word play in the poetry and to create their own using carefully chosen words and phrases. They will sometimes work collaboratively in pairs and groups. They will communicate outcomes orally and in writing (possibly including ICT).

Prior learning

Before starting this Unit check that the children can:
■ Distinguish between real words and nonsense words.
■ Notice a poem's sound and meaning.
■ Perform in unison, following the rhythm and keeping time; invent actions.
■ List words and phrases or use a word to be humorous.
If they need further support please refer to a prior Unit or a similar Unit in Year 1.

Resources

Phase 1:
Peter Piper by Anon ✸; *Good Morning, Mr Croco-Doco-Dile* by Charles Causley ✸; Photocopiable page 191 'Animal nonsense'; Interactive activity 'Animal nonsense' ✸
Phase 2:
Janny Jim Jan by Charles Causley ✸
Phase 3:
On the Ning Nang Nong by Spike Milligan ✸
Phase 4:
A short silly rhyme; *Three Little Ghostesses* by Anon ✸; *Peter Piper* by Anon ✸; *Have You Read..?* by Judith Nicholls ✸; *Conversation* by Michael Rosen ✸; *Shop Chat* by Libby Houston ✸; Photocopiable page 192 'Three wicked witchesses'; Assessment activity 'Funny poems' ✸

Cross-curricular opportunities

Art and design – Children could paint funny animals to accompany their poetry

UNIT 3 ■ Teaching sequence

Phase	Children's objectives	Summary of activities	Learning outcomes
1	I can recognise how language choices can make a poem funny. I can use inventive language to create humour in poetry.	Identify the humour in words. Test humorous verse with a smile test. Write a tongue-twister. Write lines with alliterative humour.	Children can recognise and create lines with humorous language.
2	I can respond to funny poems through pictures and drama.	Draw a picture from listening to a poem Recite a poem and add actions	Children can listen to, respond to and perform poems.
3	I can use inventive language to contribute to a class poem.	Contributing ideas for a class poem Writing, with a partner, two lines of class poem	Children understand how to play with interesting and inventive language choice to create or continue humour. Children know how to go about writing a humorous poem of their own.
4	I can recognise how language choices can make a poem funny. I can use inventive language to create humour in poetry.	Investigating a poem's humour. Planning with a response partner their own new poem. Writing and performing their own poem.	Children can write a simple poem of their own, playing with interesting and inventive language choice to create or continue particular patterns.

Provide copies of the objectives for the children.

DAY 1 ⬛ What's so funny?

Key features	Stages	Additional opportunities
	Introduction In a serious voice recite your poem to the children: *I met an Alli-Galli-Gator* *Who had an alli-smirky-smile* *And moved in an alli-wobbly-way.* Ask them: *Do you think my poem is good?*	**Phonics:** l*aw*, d*i*le **HFW:** way, some
Reasoning: explain the ways in which language is humorous	**Speaking and listening** Encourage the children to exchange views about the poem with a partner. Perhaps the words made their partner laugh? Write your poem on the board then share the children's views as a class.	
	Independent work Ask the children to work with a partner to identify why the poem seems silly. They should read it to each other and then write down the words that made them smile or laugh. Ask them to consider sounds. Are they important?	
	Plenary Share the children's views. Talk about the effect of alliteration; the use of words that are unexpected (*smirky*, *wobbly*); the juxtaposition of words that do not really make sense together.	

DAY 2 ⬛ Smile test

Key features	Stages	Additional opportunities
Enquiry: play games and assess how funny language can be in poems	**Introduction** Explain that you are going to give the children a special test – you want to find out who can keep a serious face. Children must start with a serious face. As you read something aloud to them, will their faces stay the same? Ask the children to stand up. Recite a short silly rhyme (for example, by Spike Milligan or Edward Lear) with entertaining language. Gesture to children to sit down as you see them smile. Does the language make the test hard? Now ask the children to judge how funny your jokes are. Tell them a silly joke that plays on language. For example: *What do you call a rabbit who stays in the sun too long? Answer: A hot cross bunny.*	**Phonics:** br*ea*d, p*o*le **HFW:** who, too
	Speaking and listening Ask the children to share their views with a partner, laughter-rating your joke before holding up a score for you on a individual whiteboard. Try again with a tongue-twisting rhyme, such as *Peter Piper* from the CD-ROM.	
Communication: create their own poetry using carefully chosen words and phrases	**Independent work** Ask the children, with partners, to write a silly tongue-twisting rhyme about another alliterative person (such as *Betty Batter* or *Tommy Tadpole*). **Plenary** Listen to some of the children's tongue-twisters.	

DAY 3 ■ Writing nonsense

Key features	Stages	Additional opportunities
	Introduction Display and read aloud *Good Morning, Mr Croco-Doco-Dile* from the CD-ROM. Admit that this poem inspired yours.	**Phonics:** *way, good*
Enquiry: assess how funny language can be in poems	**Speaking and listening** Ask the children to partner-read the poem. Suggest reading verses to each other to do the smile test. Ask them to list three or four words that work well. Bring the class back together and share their results. Identify alliteration. Open the 'Animal nonsense' interactive from the CD-ROM. Model how to create nonsense lines about one of the animals. Share oral ideas for others.	
Communication: create their own poetry using carefully chosen words and phrases	**Independent work** Give the children copies of photocopiable page 191 'Animal nonsense' and ask them to work independently or with a partner to write lines of silly language to suit these animals. Suggest that alliteration will be helpful. Suggest reading lines aloud to each other before their final writing.	**Support:** children can use support each other when writing **Extend:** children can write a longer poem about one of the animals
Evaluation: give feedback to others	**Plenary** Let the children read their lines. Other children may be able to suggest a useful alliterative word. Which animal gains the largest number of funny lines?	

Guided reading
Help the children to read *Good Morning, Mr Croco-Doco-Dile* from the CD-ROM. Suggest they discuss with a partner the structure and rhyme patterns they can identify.

Assessment
Talk to the children about alliteration: What is it? Challenge the children to identify six to eight examples of alliteration in *Good Morning, Mr Croco-Doco-Dile*. Refer back to the learning outcomes on page 183.

Further work
Give the children opportunities to make up some alliterative lines about household pets.

DAY 1 ▪ Painting pictures

Key features	Stages	Additional opportunities
	Introduction Read aloud *Janny Jim Jan* from the CD-ROM (without the children seeing the text).	**Phonics:** t*ie*, m*oo*r **HFW:** man, his, again
Enquiry: assess how funny language can be in poems	**Speaking and listening** Ask the children to share reactions with a partner. Did they find it amusing? Why? Compare ideas as a class. Was one word/line particularly funny?	
	Independent work Ask the children to close their eyes and let the poem's words form a picture of Janny Jim Jan in their minds as you read aloud again. Let the children put that picture onto paper.	
Communication: develop their ability to discuss word play in the poetry	**Plenary** Compare results. Ask the children to explain their pictures, justifying a detail with a reference to the poem. Emphasise that there cannot be a wrong picture as the poet wants us to form our own pictures.	

DAY 2 ▪ Funny words, funny actions

Key features	Stages	Additional opportunities
	Introduction Display and read together *Janny Jim Jan* from the CD-ROM.	**Phonics:** t*ie*, m*oo*r **HFW:** man, his, again
Reasoning: explain the ways in which language is humorous	**Speaking and listening** Invite the children to suggest words from the poem that they do not understand. Write these on the board. Ask: *What does* backsyvore *mean? What other word begins like that? Why did the poet use a word that sounds nonsense?* Point out alliteration and rhyme that makes little sense. Does the poet just want to make the reader laugh? Read it together again so the children become used to the words.	
Communication: work collaboratively in groups	**Independent work** Suggest that the poem is funniest when heard. Ask the children, in small groups, to work out how to perform it as an action rhyme.	**Support:** use mixed-ability groups for the poem performances
Evaluation: give feedback to others	**Plenary** Watch the children's performances, encouraging constructive comments.	

Guided reading
Ask the children to read *Janny Jim Jan* as a pair or in groups with your teaching assistant. Suggest they take turns reciting lines independently or in pairs.

Assessment
Read *Janny Jim Jan* aloud. Suggest that the poem seems silly. Can the children identify four reasons why the poem seems silly?
Refer back to the learning outcomes on page 183.

Further work
Extend the Assessment task by asking the children to write a children to write another silly poem about Janny Jim Jan.

DAY 1 ■ Fantasy lands

Key features	Stages	Additional opportunities
Reasoning: explain the ways in which language is humorous **Communication:** work collaboratively in pairs	**Introduction** Display and read aloud *On the Ning Nang Nong* from the CD-ROM. Discuss why this poem seems silly. Ask: *Where is the Ning Nang Nong? Do animals and trees really make these noises?* Suggest writing a class poem about another noisy fantasy land. **Speaking and listening** Encourage the children to share ideas for an alliterative place name with their partners. Compare ideas as a class, then write a first line. For example: *In the Trong, Trang, Tring.* **Independent work** Ask the children: *Who or what lives in our fantasy land?* Ask partners to agree on three inhabitants that could be funny. Compare the children's ideas, and finally list about eight fantasy creatures to have in your poem. Ask: *What noises could they make?* **Plenary** Collect and discuss ideas before making a final list. Keep a copy.	**Phonics:** *cow, mice* **HFW:** *where, tree, when*

DAY 2 ■ What a noise!

Key features	Stages	Additional opportunities
Evaluation: judge the effectiveness of their word choices **Communication:** create their own poetry using carefully chosen words and phrases **Communication:** develop their ability to discuss word play	**Introduction** Return to yesterday's list of your fantasy world's inhabitants. **Speaking and listening** Ask the children to discuss the best order with their partners. Could the noises be more original? Collect ideas and agree changes on the board. **Independent work** Put the class into small groups and allocate each group an inhabitant and its noise. The group must write two lines of the poem for the noisy inhabitant. **Plenary** Put the lines together. Make inventive suggestions, helping the children to see how language can be adventurous. Ask them: *Can we find an alliterative word? Can we make this line funnier or more surprising? How often shall we repeat the place name? What about punctuation?* Save the finished poem and have a grand class performance.	**Phonics:** *cow, mice* **HFW:** *where, tree, when* **Support:** children can make oral rather than written contributions

Guided reading

Working in groups with an adult, let the children read *On the Ning Nang Nong*. Suggest they take turns to read single or pairs of lines. Do they want to add actions?

Assessment

Read *On the Ning Nang Nong* again. Ask the children: *Can you describe two animals in this place? What is 'silly' about these animals?*
Refer back to the learning outcomes on page 183.

Further work

Progress from the assessment task to the children working in a group to create a new noisy poem, perhaps about their household pets.

DAY 1 ■ Scores on the board

Key features	Stages	Additional opportunities
	Introduction Read *Three Little Ghostesses* from the CD-ROM to the children. Mime actions as you recite the poem.	**Phonics:** three **HFW:** what, make
Enquiry: assess how funny language can be in poems	**Speaking and listening** Ask the children to share their reactions with a partner. Did they find the poem funny? Did the words tell a story? Was there something silly about it? Ask them to end their discussion by deciding on a laughter score to write on their individual whiteboards Compare class scores. What is the poem's average laughter score? Display the poem and read it aloud.	
Reasoning: explain the ways in which language is humorous	**Independent work** Ask the children to investigate the poem more closely, working out what makes its language funny. Ask them to write down four words that are silly because they are not correct words. Why has the poet used them?	
	Plenary Share the children's results. Is the poet making mistakes or just being silly? Does the title warn readers about this?	

DAY 2 ■ More word play

Key features	Stages	Additional opportunities
	Introduction Remind the children of the nonsense poem the class wrote in Phase 3. Display and read it together.	**Phonics:** three **HFW:** what, make
Communication: develop their ability to discuss word play in the poetry	**Speaking and listening** Ask the children to share views with their partners on which two lines they think use the best nonsense language. Encourage them to provide reasons. Compare some ideas as a class. Point out elements in their selections: original words, alliterative lines, inventive language. Display and read together *Three Little Ghostesses.* Explain that you want the children to write a similar poem, but called *Three Wicked Witchesses.* Stress the need to experiment before their final writing. Suggest using words ending in *ch*, and then making silly plurals – for example, *lunch* becomes *lunchesses*. Make a class list of *–ch* words: *hutch, watch, church, hatch, munch, crunch, bunch, patch, catch, latch, trench, pitch, touch, clutch, stitch.*	
Communication: create their own poetry using carefully chosen words and phrases	**Independent work** Ask the children, in pairs, to work on some silly lines for a poem about a visit by the three wicked witchesses to their school. Suggest they keep notes. **Plenary** Discuss progress. Do a class recital, with actions, of *Three Little Ghostesses.*	

DAY 3 ▪ A display of nonsense

Key features	Stages	Additional opportunities
	### Introduction Remind the children about their poem *Three Wicked Witchesses*.	**Phonics:** three **HFW:** what, make
Evaluation: give feedback to others	### Speaking and listening Ask the children to continue working, individually or with partners, to write their draft poem, using their notes from yesterday. Remind the children of how you all experimented before writing the final version of the class poem, and suggest they read lines aloud to their response partners to gain reaction and suggestions. Encourage them to think about word and line order.	**Support:** encourage children to say their lines to their partner before writing
Communication: create their own poetry using carefully chosen words and phrases	### Independent work Ask the children to write their final versions on photocopiable page 192 'Three Wicked Witchesses'. Emphasise the importance of good presentation.	
Communication: communicate outcomes orally and in writing (possibly using ICT)	### Plenary If possible, use a scanner to view some of the poems on screen. Hold a grand poetry recital session, perhaps with the children adding actions when appropriate. Finally, use the poems in a *Three Wicked Witchesses* display.	

Guided reading
Let the children work with a partner to read *Three Little Ghostesses*. Work with them to identify intentionally misspelled words. Agree how they should be spelled. If there is time, suggest they read some of the other children's poems.

Assessment
Use the 'Funny poems' photocopiable assessment activity. Children will need copies of the poems *Peter Piper*, *Have You Read..?*, *Conversation and Shop Chat* from the CD-ROM. Assess the children's recognition that the writers are playing with language. Refer back to the learning outcomes on page 183.

Further work
Extend the assessment task by asking the children to discuss and suggest other ways that these writers could have played with the language in their poems.

Animal nonsense

elephant

hippopotamus

alligator

dinosaur

rhinoceros

Three Wicked Witchesses

100 LITERACY FRAMEWORK LESSONS YEAR 2

PHOTOCOPIABLE